Walk!

Tenerife

with

Jan Kostura

and

David & Ros Brawn

DISCOVERY WALKING GUIDES LTD

Walk! Tenerife

ISBN 9781782750406

First edition published September 2006
Reprinted March 2008
Second Edition March 2012
Third Edition July 2017
Copyright © 2006, 2012, 2017

Published by
Discovery Walking Guides Ltd.
10 Tennyson Close, Northampton NN5 7HJ, England

Maps are adapted from **Tenerife Hikers' Maps**
published by **Discovery Walking Guides Ltd.**

Photographs*
Photographs in this book were provided by Jan Kostura
with additional images by Ros & David Brawn.

Front Cover Photographs

Walk 3, Los Órganos   Walk 41, Carboneras to Taganana

Walk 29, Roques de García   Walk 31, Mighty Guajara

Text and photographs* © Jan Kostura, David & Ros
Brawn 2017

Walk! Tenerife
CONTENTS

WALKS IN THE SOUTH

WALKS IN THE WEST

CENTRAL HIGH ALTITUDE ROUTES

WALKS IN THE ANAGA

After university, **Jan Kostura** set off on his travels, living and working in various far-flung places inspired by his passion for stimulating multicultural environments. However, being a stressed out desk-jockey in a hectic consulting business turned out not to be his thing, so after two years slouching in a chair he swapped the office for the more liberating environment of the great outdoors.

He found his second home in the Canary Islands, where he fell in love with the ambiance, the warm-hearted people, the constant sun, the stunning mountains and flamboyant nature.

Jan is also co-author (with Charles Davis) of **Walk! La Palma** (3rd edition) and of **Walk! La Gomera** (4th edition), both titles published by Discovery Walking Guides Ltd.

Nowadays Jan works as a mountain guide, organizing hiking expeditions and adventure holidays, and writes articles on travelling.

David & Ros Brawn moved to southern Tenerife in 1988. Finding a large resort filled with 'lost' tourists their first project was to produce the first integrated street plan of Las Américas/Los Cristianos, current editions of which continue to provide the resort mapping that everyone uses. Discovering the resort hinterland resulted in the first 'Warm Island Walking Guides' for Tenerife, then La Gomera and so Discovery Walking Guides was born.

Almost three decades later, David & Ros have hundreds of books and maps to their credit. Having pioneered the use of GPS for walkers, they've surveyed and mapped to produce the 'Tour & Trail' series of maps, 'Walk!' books and the popular 'Bus & Touring' maps. Along the way David became a member of the British Cartographic Society including contributions to its Maplines magazine.

For a full list of destinations and publications see:
www.dwgwalking.co.uk

TENERIFE - A WALKER'S ISLAND

Tenerife is a big island - 2034 square kilometres big. It offers the walker a wide variety of landscapes to choose from; everything from coastal strolls, high altitude summits, pine forests and laurel forests, challenging and strenuous routes to easy country walks.

Your choice of routes will probably be influenced by where you are based. Major roads are generally of a good standard, and public bus services are efficient, clean and reliable. Taxis are reasonable value. Even so, to travel for two or three hours to reach a walk (and back again) can be tedious, so it is best to choose your accommodation to suit your walking needs. Notes on access for each route by bus and/or car are included in each walk introduction.

THE NORTH

The original tourist area of Tenerife offers accommodation of all types around Puerto de la Cruz giving easy access to the Orotava Valley which climbs up from the north coast until it meets the northern reaches of the Parque Nacional del Teide. There are fine coastal walks in this area, most of which are clearly sign-posted and easy to follow (ask in the local Tourist Offices).

Walks 6 & 7

Our nine varied routes concentrate on the higher altitude areas around **La Caldera**, **Aguamansa**, **Pinolere** and **Montaña Limón** which offer plenty of walks through pine forests and along forest tracks and walking trails, with fine views in clear weather.

THE SOUTH

There's plenty of accommodation in the sunny southern resorts of **Los Cristianos**, **Playa de las Américas**, **Costa Adeje** and **Playa Fañabé**, and plenty of variety for walkers. We offer ten diverse routes; forest walks, mountains and *barrancos*, villages and untouched wild countryside.

We guarantee that southern Tenerife will never seem the same again.

THE WEST

Our exciting selection of eight walks includes mountain routes and rugged country hikes in this unspoiled region of the island. The west can be reached by car or bus from the northern and southern resorts, and from the west coast resort areas of **Los Gigantes**, **Playa Santiago** and **Playa de la Arena**.

Parking is limited near **Masca** for routes 25 and 26, so start out early.

CENTRAL TENERIFE

If you want to stay in the centre, there's only one choice; the **Parador Nacional**. Otherwise you can reach **Las Cañadas** by public bus from **Puerto de la Cruz** on the north coast, or from **Playa de las Américas** in the south. Drivers will usually find parking near the walking routes.

Our eight walks include some of the most exciting mountain and *cañadas* routes within the National Park, including a 'Lunar Landscape' route, as well as the challenges of 'The Big One - Crater Rim Challenge' and the ascent of **Mount Teide**.

Walk 33

Mouflon control restrictions
Authorities restrict access to several official trails in the Teide National Park
on some weekdays (May/June and October/November). On those days only,
this could affect our Walks 8, 9, 28, 29, 31, 32, 33, & 34. For details ask at
pnteide@tenerife.es, in the National Park tourist offices (El Portillo or
Parador) or in local tourist offices.

THE ANAGA

Walk 41

Never mind that it takes a bit more effort
to get to, the **Anaga** offers wild beauty,
tiny hamlets, soaring peaks and plunging
barrancos.

We guarantee that you'll never forget
walking in the remote north-east of the
island. We've extended and expanded our
routes in this most remote area of
Tenerife.

Walk 43

Our nine memorable routes
take in **Chamorga**, **Cruz del
Carmen**, **Taborno**,
Taganana, **Las Carboneras**
and more.

Visit the most remote hamlet on the island, see some of the rarest endemic
plants and experience some of the best views and most extreme geology in the
Canary Islands.

DWG's Symbols Rating Bar shows key information about a walking route in a quick glance. Remember that effort/exertion and refreshment ratings are the authors' opinions and the time shown is walking time without stops.

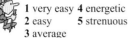

our rating for effort/exertion:

1 very easy **4** energetic
2 easy   **5** strenuous
3 average

approximate **time** to complete a walk (compare your times against ours early in a walk) - does not include stopping time

approximate walking **distance** in kilometres

 200m

850m

approximate **ascents/descents** in metres (N = negligible)

linear route, out & back

linear route, one way

circular route

figure of eight route

refreshments
May be at start or end of a route only. Rating refers to quality of refreshments, not number of choices (0=none, 5=very good)

risk of **vertigo**

Walk descriptions include: timing in minutes, shown as (40M), compass directions, shown as (NW), heights in metres, shown as (1355m) and GPS waypoints, shown as (Wp.3).

A Note About Walking Times
Walking times create more discussion than any other aspect of walking guide books. Our walking times are for *continuous walking* at an easy pace without stops, representing the quickest time you are likely to complete a route. Most of us walk at a similar pace; approx 4-6kmh. As our routes are planned as fun adventures you are unlikely to simply march along the route from start to finish. We all take stops to enjoy the views, marvel at the flora, or simply to take a break. As a result, we suggest you add 25-50% to those continuous walking times, to allow for the stops you'll make along the route.

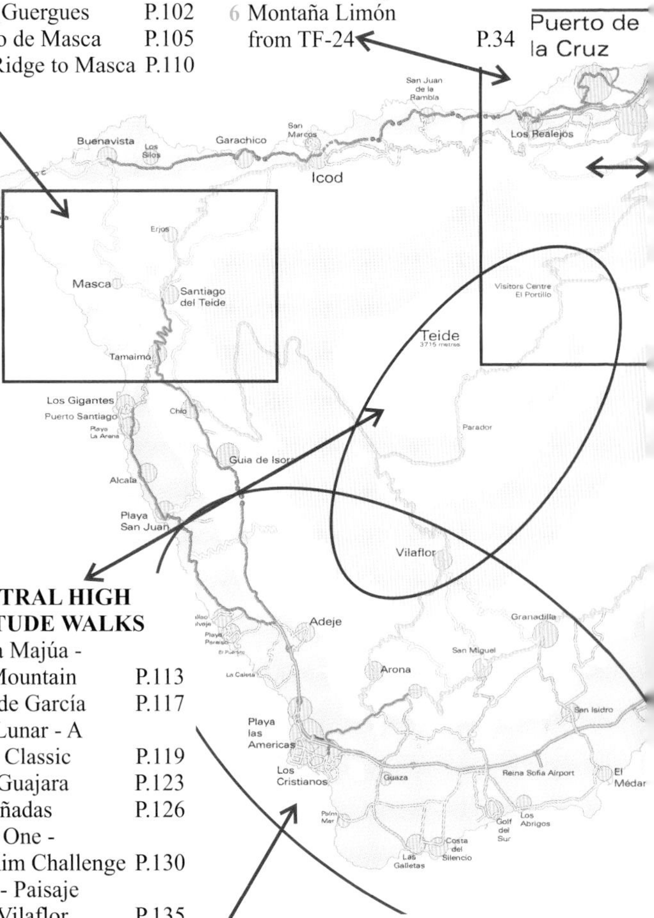

Puerto de la Cruz

San Juan de la Rambla

San Marcos

Los Realejos

Buenavista
Los Silos

Garachico

Icod

Punta Teno

Erjos

Masca

Santiago del Teide

Tamaimo

Visitors Centre El Portillo

Teide
3715 metres

Los Gigantes
Puerto Santiago
Playa La Arena

Chio

Parador

Alcalá

Guia de Isora

Playa San Juan

Vilaflor

Adeje

Granadilla

San Miguel

Arona

La Caleta

Playa las Américas

Los Cristianos

Guaza

Reina Sofía Airport

El Médano

Palm Mar

Golf del Sur
Los Abrigos

Costa del Sur

Las Galletas

Costa del Silencio

San Isidro

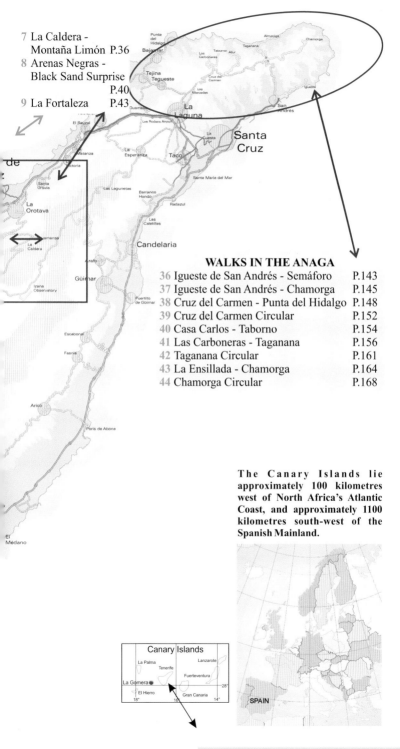

7 La Caldera -
Montaña Limón P.36
8 Arenas Negras -
Black Sand Surprise P.40
9 La Fortaleza P.43

WALKS IN THE ANAGA

36 Igueste de San Andrés - Semáforo   P.143
37 Igueste de San Andrés - Chamorga   P.145
38 Cruz del Carmen - Punta del Hidalgo   P.148
39 Cruz del Carmen Circular   P.152
40 Casa Carlos - Taborno   P.154
41 Las Carboneras - Taganana   P.156
42 Taganana Circular   P.161
43 La Ensillada - Chamorga   P.164
44 Chamorga Circular   P.168

The Canary Islands lie approximately 100 kilometres west of North Africa's Atlantic Coast, and approximately 1100 kilometres south-west of the Spanish Mainland.

The map sections used in this book have been adapted from **Tenerife Hikers'
Maps**, published by Discovery Walking Guides Ltd.

For more information on DWG publications, visit:
www.dwgwalking.co.uk

Altitude & Features

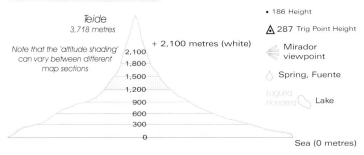

Roads, Tracks, Trails & Features

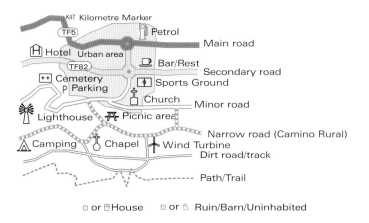

Walking Routes

Every walking route in a Walk! guidebook can be easily and reliably navigated, simply by following the detailed walk description. All of our routes are researched using a GPS so that we have an accurate record of where we have been. Even if you do not use a GPS yourself, you can be reassured that all Walk! routes have been accurately recorded.

Using a GPS with our waypoints will enable you to navigate the route with pin-point accuracy. Your GPS will show you where you are on the route in relation to the waypoints. Waypoints are provided for the key decision points on each walking route e.g. at trail junctions. Our GPS waypoints are most reassuring when you are adventuring in a new destination, as you know exactly where you are. Finding the start of a walk is simplicity itself as Waypoint 1 is at the start of each walking route.

GPS accuracy depends upon the local conditions affecting the reception of GPS signals. In the Laurel Forest, in steep *barrancos* and on cliff faces, you will get a lower standard of accuracy, though in these situations you will find there is only one obvious trail to follow. Note that at **Masca**, the absence of satellites at the horizon and the reflected signals from overhead satellites renders GPS inaccurate in this specific location.

Waypoint Lists for Walk! Tenerife are available as a free download zip file from: www.dwgwalking.co.uk/gpxDownloads.htm; simply download the zip file and unzip it into its separate waypoint files in a choice of gpx, wpt or text waypoint files.

Garmin GPS users can download the free digital Tenerife Hikers' Custom Maps on DWG's website www.dwgwalking.co.uk which will enable you to use the map as your basemap on your GPS. These Custom Maps are medium resolution (200dpi) 8bit colour images in kmz format, but are not a substitute for the printed Tenerife Hikers' Maps at 1600dpi 32 bit CMYK colour, printed on our special Super-Durable material.

If you are interested to know more about GPS, we have made **GPS The Easy Way** available as a free download at www.dwgwalking.co.uk/gps.htm.

Remember:
A Compass points North
But a GPS shows you where you are,
Shows you where you have been,
And can show you where you want to go.

1

If one route characterises walking in the **Orotava Valley**, then it has to be the 'Choza Classic'. Bus riders have the advantage over car drivers by starting at **La Caldera** but having the option to finish downhill to **La Florida** or **El Bebedero**; an easier finish than the stiff climb up through **Aguamansa** to **La Caldera**. Easy route finding combines with good scenery and bucolic charm to create one of the valley's most popular walking routes. In wet weather the steep path down the valley wall from **Choza El Topo** becomes very slippery indeed. If you get caught in wet weather, not unusual in the **Orotava Valley**, then descend on the shortest alternative route by going down the *pista* signed to **Aguamansa** - see map.

3 | 2H | 7.5 km | 320m / 320m | 3

Access by bus: Nº345 Service to **La Caldera**.

Access by car: Park at the **La Caldera** car park, off the TF-21 between kilometres 16 and 17.

Short walk alternative: to the **Aguamansa** *pista* (Wp.5), then take the *pista* down to **Aguamansa**, see map.

Our start from La Caldera (bar in view) Wp.1

We start out from the **La Caldera** car park and bus stop (Wp.1 0M) to stroll past the bar and out onto the **Pista de Mamio** (aka **Pista Monte del Pino**) (Wp.2).

Wp.2, onto Pista de Mamio

We pass **Choza de Pedro Gil** at the **Camino de Candelaria** junction (Wp.3 10M) to continue along the broad *pista*.

Choza de Pedro Gil (Wp.3)

Our route curves into and out of a small *barranco* before we come to impressively balanced giant rocks opposite a private chained-off track. **Pista de Mamio** now meanders along going gently downhill, with only occasional views through the trees, for us to pass a little-

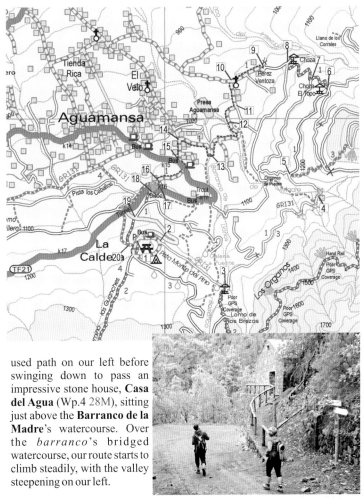

Wp.4, Casa del Agua

used path on our left before swinging down to pass an impressive stone house, **Casa del Agua** (Wp.4 28M), sitting just above the **Barranco de la Madre**'s watercourse. Over the *barranco*'s bridged watercourse, our route starts to climb steadily, with the valley steepening on our left.

Curving up to leave the valley behind, we come to the **Aguamansa** *pista* (Wp.5 35M) off to our left at a **BC 1** signpost; if you opt for this alternative, then you're now at the highest point of your route.

We continue up the **Pista de Mamio**, immediately passing a stepped trail (**GR131**) up on our right, going to **Los Órganos** (our Walk 3). It's a steady uphill, accompanied by impressive glimpses through the trees, all the way up to **Choza El Topo** (Wp.6 45M) with its *pista* and trail cross-roads. At the *choza*, a broad track climbs up to the right, an alternative **Los Órganos** route, while **Pista de Mamio** continues ahead and a broad trail drops down beside the shelter. **Choza El Topo** is a popular rest point so on weekends you'll be lucky to find the seats unoccupied.

From **Choza El Topo** we take the broad trail dropping steeply down the forested slopes. Our trail starts steep and gets steeper as we skitter down through a series of zigzags to a *pista* going left off a hairpin bend (Wp.7 51M). By now you'll have realised why we don't recommend this route in wet weather, when you are likely to slither down out of control to arrive at the bottom looking like a pig in the proverbial.

More steep zigzags bring us down to a crossroads where we meet the **Aguamansa** *pista* (Wp.8 60M). We continue downhill on the second left-hand *pista* to a beautiful view of **Pico del Teide** framed by the tall trees before dropping down to the end of a tarmac lane (Wp.9).

The lane takes us out into a bucolic landscape of farm plots and log cabins, enhanced by the flowers and white broom lining the narrow lane. Passing a concrete lane on our left, we stroll along to the shrine junction (Wp.10 69M).

The shrine at Wp.10

We turn uphill for a steady climb up past houses, heading directly towards the mighty **Órganos** rock 'pipes' to a crossroads (Wp.11). Keeping right (signed 'Aguamansa'), we stroll along the fence before coming to a signposted Y-junction (Wp.12), where we take the right branch towards pines. Easy strolling takes us past neat villas into the lush **Barranco de los Llanos**, where in the U-bend of our lane (Wp.13) a trail signed 'Casa Forestal/A.R.La Caldera' following the watercourse offers an optional finish of our route. Now it is easy strolling along the lane past the first houses to meet the **El Velo** street at **Restaurante La Vereda** (Wp.14 85M). It's seriously uphill as we turn left to climb up the steep street to come onto the TF-21 by the bus stop (Wp.15 90M) next to a big *drago*. Going left, we walk up to the **Bar/Rest Aguamansa** and give in to the temptation for refreshments before tackling the climb up to **La Caldera**.

From the bar (0M), we cross the TF-21 to take the tarmac lane beyond a vehicle barrier up to the 'La Caldera' signed trail (Wp.16) a few metres before a private gate. Climbing up through the woods, we stick to the fence as another trail forks off right to climb up to the TF-21 (Wp.17 6M) at a Km16 road marker. Carefully crossing the road, we take the path into the woods and immediately keep right for a small detour off the PR trail to climb up to a surprise - the little-known **Mirador de la Glorieta** (Wp.18) complete with seats and 'grinding wheel' table, not to mention an awesome view of the **Orotava Valley** when it isn't cloudy. Back on our path, we rejoin the PR trail, passing a fainter path off to our left for a pleasant traverse of the wooded slope along the main, well-trodden path.

Crossing the **La Caldera** access road (Wp.19), we climb through the trees to join the GR/SL trail (Wp.20). Turning left, a final short slog brings us up over steps onto the **La Caldera** car park.

An easy tour of the upper **Orotava Valley** taking in sections of classic walking trails before descending back to **La Caldera** by a little-known trail. Take your time on the strenuous climb up through the forest on the **Candelaria** trail and you'll be rewarded with easy strolling to **Choza Chimoche** plus a relaxed descent back to your start point. Should you be caught out by bad weather, or find the climb too much, there are three options to shorten this route.

* at **La Caldera**

Access by bus: Nº345 Service to **La Caldera**.

Access by car: Park at the **La Caldera** car park, off the TF-21 between kilometres 16 and 17.

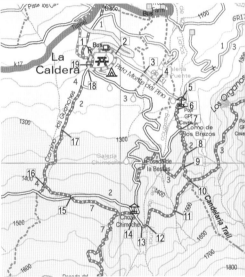

We start out from the parking area at **La Caldera** (Wp.1 0M) (see photo of Wp.1 at beginning of Walk 1 description) to stroll past the bar and round to the junction with the main *pista forestal* (Wp.2) signed 'Los Organos'. It's an easy stroll down the broad **Pista de Mamio** (aka **Pista Monte del Pino**) passing a water pipeline and a walking trail crossing our route (Wp.3).

Over a bridge, we pass a rough forest trail off to our right (Wp.4) to pass a trail off to the left just before the **Choza de Pedro Gil** and *fuente* at the 'Camino de Candelaria' signed junction (Wp.5 10M). Here we leave the *pista* to follow the clear signed **Candelaria** trail up into the forest.

Three crosses at Wp.6

Now we cross a watercourse and then we are into a relentless ascent through the pines and tree heather, gentle at first as we come up to pass the three crosses (Wp.6 12M) but then getting steeper as we zigzag up the valley wall. You'll need a top-notch GPS unit to keep satellite signals amongst all these trees and the steep valley wall, not that

there's any danger of getting lost as there is just one clear path and we are on it.

Taking breaks whenever we need them, we gradually ascend up through the twists and turns to come to a clearer area by some large eucalyptus trees and a discreet shrine set in the crook of a hairpin bend. Just a little more climbing brings us up onto a *pista forestal* at **Lomo de los Brezos** (Wp.7 25M) for a welcome break. You can shortcut the route at this point by going right on the *pista* and at a T-junction go right again to head down to **La Caldera**; see map.

Across the track, we go up onto a small walking trail which winds up amongst the trees in a series of zigzags. As usual, it is onwards and upwards on the relentless ascent, the magnificent **Los Órganos** cliffs glimpsed through the trees on our left providing some light relief. There is so little to comment on in this bland section of forest that even a small rock outcrop (Wp.8) seems like a major feature, before we come up to an unmarked junction (Wp.9 40M). Here a broad earth path sweeps gently down into the valley on our right, our second opportunity to short cut back to **La Caldera**.

Motivated by pleasant sunny weather, we continue uphill through the thinning pines to climb into a region of black *picón* where our path goes up through a narrow trench before coming to a crossroads of trails (Wp.10 45M). Here the **Los Órganos** trail comes in from the left while the **Candelaria** pilgrimage route continues straight up ahead of us.

Eroded gullies between Wps.11-13

We go right, leaving the pilgrimage path, gradient easing for us to climb gently above a tree-filled ravine. Our path undulates along to cross a picturesque rocky watercourse (Wp.11 50M) and a series of watershed gullies. Now our route runs gently downhill as it swings south.

Crossing the watercourse (Wp.12 56M), we round a ridge into a gentler valley to cross a pair of watercourses to come onto the end of a dirt track (Wp.13).

Choza Chimoche (Wp.14)

Following the track, we come along to **Choza Chimoche** at a junction of tracks set in a forest clearing (Wp.14 59M), often so popular that you might be lucky to get a seat.

From the *choza* we can go north (N) on the right hand *pista* to descend the broad dirt track past **Galería Chimoche** to **La Caldera**; our third opportunity to shortcut.

From **Choza Chimoche** we head west (W) along the track which gently climbs. Ten minutes from **Choza Chimoche**, when the track runs through a shallow S-bend, a walking trail (easy to miss!) branches right off the *pista* (Wp.15 68M), marked 'La Caldera' by a small sign up on the pine tree - if you miss this junction, you can take the next right fork 250 metres later which rejoins our route at Wp.16.

Stepping off the *pista*, we come down into the green wood on a trail, unfortunately littered with stones making for slow progress, then bear right at a Y-junction of trails (Wp.16 72M). Although technically part of the same forest this is a softer, greener woodland compared to the harsh pines and tree heather on the ascent up the **Candelaria** path. Our trail twists down through the trees in a steady descent, the trees closing over our route to form a green tunnel (77M).

After the green tunnel the woodland opens up as we cross a small watercourse, and the path is less rock-littered. Continuously descending, we come down to cross a water pipeline (Wp.17 92M), the woodland less dense around our route for a short section. Laurel trees supplement the Canarian pines and tree heathers as we continue down alongside moss-covered rocks to come to the end of the trail, signed on a large pine, at a dirt track (102M).

Going left, we come down the rocky track to cross the **La Caldera** ring road (Wp.18), straight over onto a woodland path which takes us through the wood, passing a path off to our right, where we join a fence (Wp.19) beside which we come down onto the tarmac again at the parking area (105M continuous walking).

3

Northern Tenerife has one true classic walk, and this is it. Following an amazing woodland and ravine trail, we traverse the south-east wall of the **Orotava Valley**, taking in a surfeit of scenery, views, flora and orogenical geology. You need good weather, surefootedness and an adequate fitness level, but if you have these, then this is one route not to miss.

There are short exposed stretches on the **Órganos** trail (Wp.9 to Wp.20), most are fitted with fixed ropes. The trail is reasonably broad at all times. On the most exposed stretch where our trail traverses a sheer cliff, the well fixed steel-pipe handrail has been complemented by a sturdy reliable railing.

Although this route was officially closed for over two years due to landslips, as of 2017, this spectacular *sendero* is officially open again. The **Órganos** trail is prone to landslips, when the authorities place temporary closure barriers at Wp.9&20.

The **Órganos** trail should not be attempted in bad weather or after heavy rains.

* at **La Caldera**

Access by bus: Nº345 service to **La Caldera**.

Access by car: Park at the **La Caldera** car park, off the TF-21 between kilometres 16 and 17.

From the **La Caldera** car park (Wp.1 0M) (see photo of Wp.1 at beginning of Walk 1 description) we follow the **GR131** signed 'Casa del Agua/Mamio' past the bar/rest, bearing straight ahead onto the broad **Pista de Mamio** (aka **Pista Monte del Pino**) (Wp.2 3M) signed 'Los Organos'.

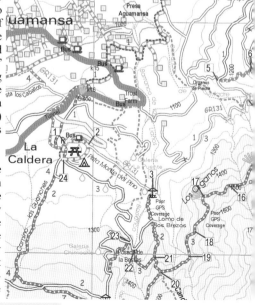

We pass the **Choza de Pedro Gil** (Wp.3 12M) path junction where **Camino de Candelaria** climbs steeply to our right. Passing the balanced rocks and private *pista* we drop down below an eroded rock face and past **Casa del Agua** (Wp.4 35M) to cross the stone bridge, then labouring up the steady ascent to the 'Aguamansa' signed *pista*.

Views before Wp.5

Now the real exertions begin. Twenty metres past the *pista*, a stepped trail signed 'Siete Fuentes 17km' climbs up into the forest (Wp.5 42M). Sticking to the **GR131** we climb steeply up through the pines and tree heather in a 'puff and grunt' ascent through hairpin bends before emerging onto the broad track coming up from **Choza El Topo** (Wp.6 57M).

If walking the route in reverse, we recommend using this *pista* rather than the steep woodland trails.

Through the rock gate just before Wp.9

Going right for 15 metres, we ignore a track forking right to step onto a trail which climbs on log steps up from the *pista*. Again, it is steeply up through the pines and heather, as the trail brings us up to a small stone bench (Wp.7 66M) amongst mature pines. Our path seems to get even steeper as we labour up, relieved by panoramic views of **Teide**. We're climbing steeply, skirting the forest track on our left, before coming onto a broad *lomo*, where our trail levels off to pass a **GR131** signpost (Wp.8 86M). The broad, stone-lined trail follows the clearly defined crest, then narrows down and begins to climb steeply again.

We are back to a 'puff and grunt' steep climb going up through zigzags to a long climbing traverse which brings us to a 'rock gate' immediately after which our path swings sharp right and we reach a junction of walking trails (Wp.9 95M).

Going right, we leave the **GR131** to take the level trail and are rewarded with a pleasant woodland path which contours along with magnificent views before starting to descend below a cliff to a couple of hairpin bends. Our trail drops down before our steep descent runs out for us to cross a short section with a steel rope handrail (Wp.10 115M).

After the handrail section we cross the ravine's two watercourses, between which we take care as the trail is mildly exposed. We turn into another ravine, dropping down to cross its watercourse, then climbing out to come into a most unusual ravine with a 'rock boulder river' (Wp.11 120M) falling from the heights above us, steeply down the valley wall.

The steep valley of **Barranco de la Madre** widens out as we meander along a steady ascent, curving left to resume progress along the valley wall. We zigzag up to a higher level to continue westwards (W), the high altitude woodland and ravine path having some areas of unprotected drops, but not seriously vertiginous here.

We pass a cairn-marked path (Wp.12 131M), dropping down the crest to **Casa del Agua** after which our trail swings south (S). We drop down to cross another steep ravine (Wp.13 137M) and climb again before our path starts descending through hairpin bends in lazy zigzags to bring us down to a rock viewpoint overlooking **Aguamansa** (Wp.14 143M).

From the *mirador* we continue downhill on the rock and shale surface to turn into a pocket in the valley wall where we come below a huge knob of rock. We cross the cutting's first watercourse by a pair of boulders and then cross the second watercourse directly beneath the huge knob of rock. Due to the mountainous landscape, GPS coverage is unstable in this section as our path climbs beneath steep cliffs, carefully passing a narrow landslip-prone section of path above a rock slide.

Wp.15 on the stunning rock ledge

A rock ledge curves out of sight beneath overhanging cliffs (Wp.15 153M), but don't worry. A securely fixed steel pipe plus a sturdy wooden railing protect hikers on this exposed section above a precipitous drop.

Just round the corner we step off the ledge back onto a normal width trail for a short climb up to a small rock promontory. Access to this promontory is barred by stones but shortly after we come to an even more spectacular promontory.

There's still some climbing to be done, as our trail undulates along the valley wall (poor GPS coverage in places), crossing a ravine's watercourse to pass a faint, cairn marked, path (Wp.16 164M), climbing to the left along the spur.

Further on we pass a trig point (Wp.17 171M) at a beautiful picnic setting on a rock shelf, just behind which, off the trail, is an exposed promontory with stunning views over the valley and **Pico del Teide**. Staying on the trail we turn down into a ravine, the trees clearing again for more views, after which our trail becomes a rough rocky descent of long lazy zigzags to cross a ravine's watercourse (Wp.18 185M). We then pass a narrow stretch under an eroded cliff with a fixed steel rope (Wp.19 189M) just before crossing the next ravine, where three steep valleys meet, each stuffed with endemic trees and plants; unusual in this rocky landscape.

Just past the ravine we come to face a long slope. Trudging up the steep incline, we finally arrive at the trail crossroads with the **Camino de Candelaria** and our 'Chimoche Loop' route (Wp.20 195M).

Going right we swing downhill on the pine needle covered trail running in a cutting. 180 metres after the crossroads, we come to an unmarked path junction (Wp.21 198M), very easy to miss.

On the trail after Wp.20

We could continue straight down the **Candelaria** trail to meet the *pista* and our outward route at **Choza de Pedro Gil**, but we're looking for a less skittery descent, so we go left at the junction to descend on a pleasant woodland trail above a gentle valley; when compared to the orogenical landscape earlier. Coming to a junction, we take the lower path to the right which winds down through the woods, our path becoming more trench-like as we descend before we drop down onto a *pista* (Wp.22 209M).

Lomo de los Brezos is to the right as we go left to climb up to the junction of tracks at **Pasada de las Bestias** (Wp.23 211M). Keeping straight ahead, we are on the *pista* which descends from **Choza Chimoche**, unremarkable except that we have a fast, easy walking descent through the forest, passing a campsite to cross the **La Caldera** ring road (Wp.24 234M). Across the tarmac, we follow the trail alongside the fence through the woods, then step down onto the end of the **La Caldera** car park (237M, actual walking time excluding breaks).

4

An inspiring half-day walk, which offers plenty of diversity in a relatively small area, taking in both pine forest and a fine example of the ancient *laurisilva*, with great views over the valley and of course, **Teide**. The second half of the walk follows the **GR131 - Camino de Chasna** that connects two sides of the island (more precisely two different worlds), a route of significant historical importance for the pilgrims and muleteers of the past times.

* at La Caldera

Access by bus: Nº345 service to **La Caldera**.

Access by car: Park at the **La Caldera** car park, off the TF-21 between kilometres 16 and 17.

We start from the **La Caldera** car-park/bus terminus (see the start of Walk 1). Opposite the mapboard for 'Sendero SL TF 81', we take the unmarked trail (S) between the fence and the road, starting with four stone steps (Wp.1 0M).

The stone steps at Wp.1

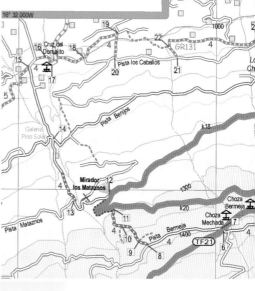

We are beside the fence on our left for 50 metres before bearing right at a Y-junction. Crossing the ring road (Wp.2 2M), we continue on a track signed 'Camino de los Guanches' on a tree trunk. A rough track takes us through the growths of *fayal-brezal*. When the track swings left we continue straight ahead (Wp.3 7M) (signed 'Sendero') along a broad trail lined by stones.

The clearly defined trail, either lined by stones or low walls runs in a shallow trench for a while.

26 Walk! Tenerife

We ignore a stone-barred trail to the right, continuing straight ahead before crossing a thick water pipe. A short stretch of bare rock gives way to soil and stones while we climb steadily. Zig-zagging up in a trench like cutting, we emerge at a Y-junction of trails (Wp.4 28M) with a cairn in the middle of the junction.

Taking the steeper right branch, we climb onto the broad **Pista Chimoche** (Wp.5 30M). Turning right, we follow the dirt road (W), passing a concrete fountain and a left-hand track shortly before coming to the TF-21 main road (Wp.6 45M). Turning right, we follow the road (NE) for 70 metres to go left (W) onto **Pista La Bermeja** (Wp.7 46M). We follow the dirt road (signed 'VM 11'), which traverses the shrubby slope with excellent views of **Teide** in front of us.

120 metres after a broader stretch allowing cars to turn around, and about the same distance before the pine forest line in front of us, we take a rough trail which forks off to the right (easily overlooked) by a pile of orange and black boulders (Wp.8 56M). The stone-littered trail is partly overgrown and after 100 metres we branch left at a Y-junction by a pile of wood (Wp.9 58M).

Our rough trail right; easily overlooked (Wp.8)

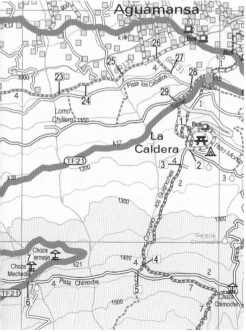

Three minutes later at a T-junction (Wp.10 61M), we carry straight on, ignoring the left-hand ascending trail. The partially grassy trail then drops more steeply, the main road below coming into view as we skirt a stand of pine. Our trail swings right in front of the pines and becomes a bit overgrown, dwindling to a path just before it emerges on the main road (Wp.11 66M).

Turning left, we stroll down the road to come to the spacious **Mirador de Mataznos** (Wp.12 71M), with its two mapboards. Turning left, we take the **Pista Mataznos**, following the **VM 14** for

'Chanajiga/Cruz de Luis'. 4 minutes later we pass a right-hand dirt track closed with a barrier, and a stone concrete fountain, 100 metres after which (after the last of the pines), we branch right onto a discreet trail (Wp.13 77M), just when the dirt road swings left.

Our trail drops steadily (NNW) through tall *fayal-brezal* and passes, partially in a trench, a natural viewpoint, before coming onto the **Pista de Benijos** (Wp.14 86M). Here we cross our Walk 5. For an easy finish you can turn right to follow the *pista* with Walk 5's description.

The 'ruler' track (Wps.14 to 15)

Crossing the *pista* we follow a trail that broadens to a track, dropping in a straight line as if designed with a ruler! We come out of the forest to a surprising fairy-tale like setting on a meadow (actually a potato field), our track being neatly lined by ferns on each side. The track becomes concreted and passes a blue gated house before being joined by the **GR131** from the left (Wp.15 95M) at which point the track disrupts its linear descent by swinging right (NE). We now follow the **GR131 Camino de Chasna** all the way to **La Caldera**.

Wp.17, the Cruz del Dornajito

Keeping straight ahead at a T-junction sixty metres later, where the concrete track branches left, we follow the dirt track to the end of the field (Wp.16 97M), where a woodland path descends on natural steps to a welcoming rest area on a meadow, the **Cruz del Dornajito** (Wp.17 99M).

From the shelter on the meadow, we take the stepped path and climb to cross a tarmac lane. The woodland path joins a sturdy covered canal as we get deeper into the beautiful forest, birds chattering. Crossing a dirt track next to a small concrete structure (Wp.18 105M), we stick to the canal before crossing it to descend on log steps.

Our path joins the covered canal

After a while we shadow a steel pipe on our right and come to a T-junction (Wp.19 111M), where we turn sharp right (S). Climbing steadily on a trail of moss and mud, we re-cross the canal, before coming onto a *pista*, 20 metres along which we climb to a Y-junction of tracks (Wp.20 117M).

Turning left (E), we follow **Pista Los Caballos** in higher *fayal-brezal*, several minutes later passing a fence with a decorative stone gate with a wheel set in it. 50 metres after crossing a broad ravine, we turn left onto a woodland path (Wp.21 125M). Going down the path we cross a thin red pipe before bearing right at a forest junction (Wp.22 128M), taking the gently ascending branch. Our path briefly joins a fence several minutes later to cross a watercourse before joining the green **SL TF 81** trail at a junction (Wp.23 140M). Keeping straight ahead, we continue on a pleasant path to come to a T-junction (Wp.24 144M), bearing right on the broader branch waymarked a bit later on a stone.

The path joins a fenced garden of a white house, then passes its back gate before passing an orange-painted house. 160 metres later, we continue straight ahead at a T-junction of paths on the corner of another fenced garden (Wp.25 151M). Our path along the fence takes us past a big entrance gate, where we join a dirt track. We pass a fruit garden, then ignore a left-hand tarmac lane to come to a T-junction at a green house with decorative stones set in its plaster (Wp.26 156M). Here we have choice of two finish routes.

If you came by bus, a good option is to continue straight ahead to finish the hike in **Aguamansa**. After 350 metres you'll descend onto the main road, where there are two restaurants and a bus stop a little down the road, with a more frequent bus service than the one from **La Caldera**.

We bear right to finish the route in **La Caldera**. We cross a thin pipe concreted into a step about a half-way before rejoining the **Pista Los Caballos** (Wp.27 160M). Bearing left, we follow the dirt track past a white cross until a path forks left off the track just when it swings sharp right (Wp.28 164M). 30 metres up the path we bear right at a junction to come through the S-shaped stone wall onto the **Pista de Benijos** (Wp.29 168M).

Crossing the *pista* we walk through the tunnel under the main road before broad stone stairs take us up just before the **La Caldera** access road. The path swings right (S) and climbs through the forest to take us back to the **La Caldera** car-park (178M).

Wp.29, crossing the Pista de Benijos

5

An **Orotava Valley** descent route, well-suited for hikers seeking tranquillity and purity, this quiet stretch of the **GR131 Camino de Chasna** leads predominantly through pristine forests - pine in its first section with two stunning natural viewpoints, *laurisilva* in the second. The admittedly monotonous second part of the route can be avoided by combining with our Walk 4, adding more variety and some metres of climbing to this downhill itinerary. The **GR131** is well waymarked, making it difficult to get lost unless you really want to.

To connect with Walk 4: stay on the **GR131** at Wp.21, at which point this Walk 5 leaves it, by taking the straight forward level dirt road (**Pista de Benijos**) towards **La Caldera**. You would connect with Walk 4 just before **Cruz del Dornajito**. Or follow this itinerary until Wp.22, 90 metres after which it is crossed by Walk 4 directly.

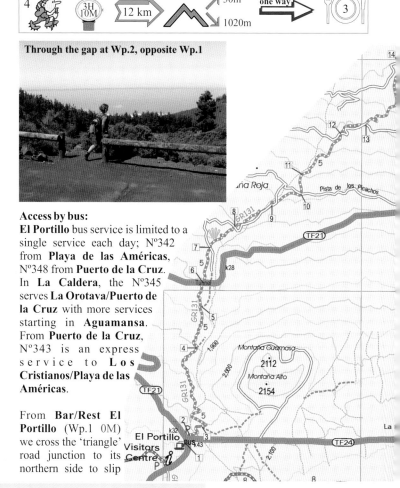

Through the gap at Wp.2, opposite Wp.1

Access by bus:
El Portillo bus service is limited to a single service each day; Nº342 from **Playa de las Américas**, Nº348 from **Puerto de la Cruz**. In **La Caldera**, the Nº345 serves **La Orotava/Puerto de la Cruz** with more services starting in **Aguamansa**. From **Puerto de la Cruz**, Nº343 is an express service to **Los Cristianos/Playa de las Américas**.

From **Bar/Rest El Portillo** (Wp.1 0M) we cross the 'triangle' road junction to its northern side to slip through a gap in the crash barriers (Wp.2 1M). Turning right, we take a path (E) alongside the crash barrier toward a mapboard visible from the gap. Passing a metal 'turnstile' we follow the path snaking through *retama* (white broom) and *rosalillo de cumbr*e, before coming to the **Alto de Guamaso** junction (Wp.3 5M).

Bearing left, we descend on a broad path and leave the national park (boundary signpost) before entering a sparse pine forest. Zig-zagging down the path, we pass a sheet of rock before coming to a Y-junction (Wp.4 23M), where we bear left (waymarked). We descend through a landscape of sparse pines, jagged rock formations and lava boulders, passing a short stretch of a donkey trail before bearing left again at the next Y-junction (Wp.5 32M).

A few minutes later broad stone stairs take us down under the TF-21 road (Wp.6 37M). On the other side we continue our gentle descent along a comfortable, wide trail. A track visible through the pines runs parallel on our right hand side before we cross it (Wp.7 44M) and come to a stunning viewpoint of the **Orotava Valley**, standing on the edge of a savage ravine.

A minute later another great viewpoint offers different scenery, this time of the upper part of the wild *barranco*. 100 metres later we cross a dirt track (Wp.8 50M) and keep descending, keeping near the ravine's edge.

Stunning viewpoint after Wp.7

We briefly rejoin the dirt track before our trail leaves it to the left to come to a shallow watercourse in a small clearing. We leave the watercourse a minute later joining a dirt track for a few metres then taking a stepped trail on the left (Wp.9 59M), at this point facing rugged rocks in distance. 100 metres later we rejoin the track briefly, before bearing right onto a wayposted trail. We cross a watercourse twice before crossing the **Pista de los Picachos** (Wp.10 65M), then cross a watercourse again to join a dirt track. A minute later, at a point where we see a T-junction 20 metres before us and also have a view of a rock overhang, we turn right onto a path (Wp.11 68M).

We soon find ourselves on a stretch of donkey trail and lava grit, while we skirt a ravine on our left. Passing a lava field, we cross a rocky ravine bed and continue on a neat woodland trail.

This comes to a dirt track (Wp.12 79M), which we cross, then briefly rejoin it in its right hand bend.

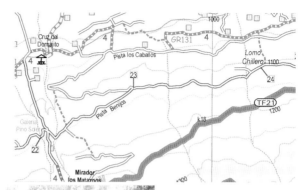

Joining another dirt track (Wp.13 84M) just a few metres below a T-junction on our right, we shortly cross a watercourse on a small meadow before re-entering the forest. Crossing a rocky bed of a ravine, we bear right onto a trail at a Y-junction two hundred metres later (Wp.14 93M).

Crossing the dirt track near a water change point (Wps.15-16)

It then crosses a broad gritty track and 5 minutes later the **Pista Bermeja** (Wp.15 100M), marked as orange 'BC 1.8'. One minute later we cross another dirt track by a GR signpost. After 200 metres we cross a piped canal (Wp.16 108M).

We then continue down the stream bed for a while before recovering our path. Crossing a watercourse, we are in deeper forest on a mostly level path. 50 metres before a dirt track visible in front of us, we bear right on a less distinct path (Wp.17 111M), heading toward a cairn and a waymark. Crossing the dirt track, we continue along the path which then crosses a narrower track (Wp.18 114M) and leads into a thick forest of young pines. The landscape changes to a mixture of pines, junipers and cistus as we come to cross the gravel track **Pista Mataznos** (Wp.19 120M).

Our path runs through growths of shrubs too tall for views and passes a wooden bench before crossing a gritty track (Wp.20 129M), while our trail broadens to a track. 100 metres later we come onto a dirt road at **Morro Quemado** by an orange-marked waypost **BC 1** (Wp.21 131M). We leave the GR route which continues straight on (connecting later with our Walk 4) and turn right, taking the broad **Pista de Benijos**.

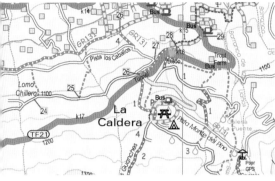

For the following 4 kilometres (until the crossroads with the **GR131**) it is a simple if a bit monotonous stroll on the dirt road, contouring along and following signposts for 'La Caldera'. At a T-junction after 600 metres we carry straight on.

We pass a green house at the **Galería Pino Soler** (Wp.22 141M), 90 metres after which we come to a discreet crossroads with a trail: this is our Walk 4; for a more interesting optional finish that follows trails rather than tracks and adds at least some ascent to the itinerary, turn left and follow the description of Walk 4. In this itinerary we stay with the dirt road for a straight forward finish. After passing a barred track on our right, landscape changing to *laurisilva*, we keep straight at a Y-junction (Wp.23 151M), then after 1.2km at **Lomo Chillero** (Wp.24 167M) straight on again.

The green **SL TF 81** joins the track here from our left. Passing a green **SL TF 81.1** junction for 'Camino La Orilla' (Wp.25 172M), we eventually come to a crossroads with the **GR131** by a road tunnel (Wp.26 179M), where we meet Walk 4.

Wp.26; crossroads with Walk 4 and GR131

Going through the tunnel to our right, we can finish our hike at *área recreativa* **La Caldera**, with its café and a bus terminus, although bus services are less frequent than from **Aguamansa**. We bear left, following the **GR131** along a pleasant woodland path.

After 250 metres the GR forks off to the left (Wp.27 183M) while we continue straight on alongside a pipe to come to a fence, along which we descend onto a tarmac lane in front of a gate (Wp.28 186M). Turning right, we stroll down the lane to the main road, emerging opposite of the **Restaurante Aguamansa** (Wp.29 189M). Another restaurant and the bus stop for **La Orotava/Puerto de la Cruz** are 100 metres down to the left.

6

This short excursion provides an alternative to the classic ascent from **La Caldera** (Walk 7) and is suitable for car drivers (no bus connection) or for those preferring a short walk with a lot of reward. The at-first-glance-indistinct flat-topped peak of **Montaña Limón** is surprisingly one of the most rewarding summits for its spectacular panoramic views of the national park, including **Teide** and on a good day the whole **Orotava Valley**.

Looking towards the mountain just after Wp.2

On the return, consider a small detour to explore the spectacular canyon rim on the north-eastern flanks of the mountain; see the end of text.

Access by car: The starting point is at an unmarked dirt parking on the **La Esperanza - El Portillo** road, Km34.5 of the TF-24.

Our start at Wp.1

From the dirt parking along the road (Wp.1 0M), we cross the crash barrier, staying on the same side of the road and cross the small crest beyond which we join a trail. This we follow to the left (SW) for 300 metres until coming to a signposted T-junction (Wp.2 5M), where we turn sharp right (N).

The flat-topped peak of **Montaña Limón** is now right in front of us as we traverse a slope on the red trail. Our trail swings left toward telescopes, while below us a dirt road and a steel barrier comes into our view.

We descend on the red-and-brown trail surrounded by shrubs to come to a mapboard and a dirt road (Wp.3 18M). Crossing the dirt road, we follow the path for 180 metres before briefly joining the dirt road, about 50 metres south-west of the steel barrier. Bearing left, we follow the *pista* for sixty metres (NW) before branching off to the right onto a trail (Wp.4 22M) into shrubs. We bear toward the visible peak of **Montaña Limón**, already spotting the distinct stone-lined *picón* trail, which follows the gentle ridgeline onto the summit.

Five minutes later we come to a crossroads of trails at the foot of the stone-littered slope of **Montaña Limón**, resembling a T-junction rather than a crossroads as just three of the branches are well-defined (Wp.5 27M). Bearing straight ahead (NNW), we follow the clear trail along the gradual ridge and climb onto the summit of

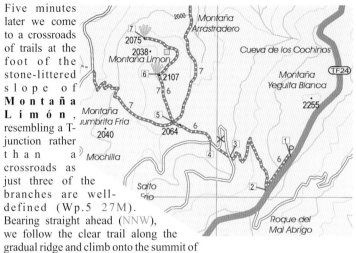

Montaña Limón with a distinct lava outcrop (Wp.6 35M). From this point, a northern summit on the other side of the forested *caldera* comes into our view.

To get to the northern summit see Walk 7 for directions. From the northern summit (Wp.7 47M), fantastic panorama views of the **Orotava Valley** open up on a clear day.

Montaña Limón in winter

We return the same way to our starting point (95M).

However, it is well worth exploring the nearby spectacular canyon to the north-east of the 'lemon' mountain. Turning left at Wp.5 (NE then N) the trail soon runs into growths of *retama* and passes an impressive natural rock gate on the right hand side. Continue for two hundred metres along or near the canyon rim to enjoy the most of the impressive scenery. Check Walk 7 Wps.9-10 for details.

7

Forests, ravines, canyons, lava dunes, plains and stunning views - this route has everything for a spectacular day trip! Starting from **La Caldera** (busy on weekends), we climb through refreshing pine forest into the national park to one of the most rewarding summits that offers spectacular 360° views.

The section of the walk between waypoints 9 and 10 follows an exposed rim of a canyon, but since it is always possible to keep away from the rim off the path, a good head for heights is not essential.

* at **La Caldera**

Access by bus: Service Nº345 drops you off at **La Caldera**. Check detailed timetable as some of the buses end prematurely in **Aguamansa**.

Access by car: Park at the **La Caldera** car park, off the TF-21 between kilometres 16 and 17.

We start from the **La Caldera** car-park/bus terminus. Opposite the **SL TF 81** mapboard we take the unmarked trail (S) between the fence and the road, starting with four stone steps (Wp.1 0M) to shadow the fence on our left for 50 metres before bearing right at a Y-junction away from the fence.

Our start at Wp.1

Crossing the road (Wp.2 2M), we continue on the 'Camino de los Guanches'. The rough, stone-littered track takes us through *fayal-brezal*, to a junction where the track swings left while we go straight ahead (Wp.3 7M) along a broad trail lined by stones. Our trail, lined by stones or low walls runs in a shallow trench for a while.

We ignore a stone-barred trail to the right, continuing straight ahead before crossing a thick water pipe. A short stretch of bare rock gives way to soil and stones while we steadily climb. Zigzagging up in a trench like cutting, we emerge at a cairned Y-junction of trails (Wp.4 28M), where our Walks 7 and 4 diverge.

Bearing left (SE) our trail traverses a wooded slope, we cross a gully and climb out to cross the **Pista Chimoche** (Wp.5 34M). Our trail continues 15 metres to the right, a 'Montaña Limón' sign confirming our route (see photo on next page). The needle-carpeted trail lined by stones meanders in the fresh pine forest. One minute after crossing three consecutive gullies, we come to an important cairn-marked T-junction of trails (Wp.6 44M), where straight on is our return way toward **Choza Chimoche**, but now we face some climbing ahead of us!

Our trail just after Pista Chimoche (Wp.5)

Bearing right (SW) through a 'gate' of stumpy posts, we follow cairns, our trail broadening to a track and climbing in switchbacks in the pleasant wood. The track narrows back to a trail and at a left bend we come to a special viewpoint with a majestic rock cleft in a sheer cliff. After the viewpoint we take the left-hand track barred by line of stones, while the trail continues straight on (they eventually merge). The track soon dwindles to a broad trail and about 50 metres later, at a T-junction, we keep left again, sticking to the edge of the valley. Climbing along the track, we come to another *mirador* viewpoint of the valley (5 metres to the left off the track).

20 metres after the *mirador* at a cairn we may take a steeper shortcut trail to the left, which 5 minutes later rejoins the track. Making our way up, the track briefly splits then merges in a right bend just before emerging past a steel barrier on a dirt road at **Pasada del Fraile** (Wp.7 70M) by a stone pillar.

Crossing the dirt road, we climb steadily in switchbacks along the track before coming to a Y-junction by several cairns (Wp.8 83M), where from our right we will later return along the dirt track to close the upper loop of the route. Now we turn left (S) taking the trail, not clearly defined, but at least dotted by small cairns as we meander up to come to a trail-crossroads on a rock shelf, where we keep straight ahead. 10 metres later we cross a watercourse and make our way along the rough stone-littered trail, which after several minutes becomes pine covered to give us some relief underfoot. We pass a lava field in a clearing, gradually approaching the rim of a canyon before joining it to come out of the forest to a stunning viewpoint of the canyon on a sheer cliff (Wp.9 105M).

Our trail now continues along the rim, some caution needed. Climbing along a rock shelf then lava surface, we are back in the wood two minutes later, keeping a safe distance (10-15 metres) from the rim. Passing a 'Parque Nacional' limits sign, we are at the rim again, rough lava crunching underfoot. 100 metres after the sign we come onto a lava plain with our first views of **Izaña** observatory; here we are in line with the head of the canyon, a majestic rock 'gate'.

Winding through growths of the white broom, the telescopes of **Izaña** come into sight. When the *retama* growths become sparser and we pass a black dune on our left, a not-too-distinct dirt track goes straight while we keep more to the right, virtually pathless at this stage, our direction defined by the telescopes on the horizon ahead. Walking exactly towards the telescopes (SSW), we skirt the summit cone of **Montaña Limón** on our right, maintaining the distance to the slope. We walk across a broad field of fine lava grit and catch first glimpses of **Pico del Teide**.

When **Teide**'s whole cone comes into view our path turns slightly right, **Teide** now being our main bearing (SW) before coming to a T-junction (Wp.10 125M), actually a trail-crossroads.

Bearing right (NNW), we take the clear trail along the gradual ridge and climb onto the summit of **Montaña Limón** with its distinct lava outcrop (Wp.11 133M). From this point, a northern summit on the other side of the forested *caldera* comes into our view. On a good day, when the **Orotava Valley** is not covered by clouds brought in by the trade winds, it is well worth continuing to the northern summit for views of the complete valley.

Wp.11 on the summit

To get to the northern summit, we do not descend to the forested caldera floor, but turn right (NE) and skirt the rim of the caldera. The red trail drops as we circle the mountain. It's worth noting the way to the northern summit through the short section of pine forest from here. The indistinct trail swings left (NW) and passes a ruin on our left just before coming into the pine forest. Maintaining direction in the forest (virtually pathless), we come out a hundred metres later with the northern summit and its cairn ahead. From the northern summit (Wp.12 145M), panoramic views of the **Orotava Valley** open up on a clear day.

We retrace our steps to Wp.10 where we turn right to follow the neat trail (W) lined by lava stones. After a section of barren lava plains we come into shrubs when our trail swings slightly to the right and starts to descend toward a pine forest. Coming into the sparse wood (Wp.13 173M), we pass a **Nº34** mapboard to descend in switchbacks on a broad *picón* trail before coming to a crossroads with a dirt road (Wp.14 181M), marked with a blue-striped wooden pole. Turning right, we follow the broad *pista* which at first runs level, then descends gently before coming to a Y-junction of *pistas* (Wp.15 202M), where we turn sharp right, following the blue marked **VM 11** for 'Ramón Caminero'. A little over 10 minutes later at a Y-junction (Wp.16 214M), the **VM 11** swings sharp left to **Ramón Caminero**, while we bear right onto a dirt track that shortly becomes increasingly rough. After 250 metres we rejoin our outward route at Wp.8.

Letting gravity do its job we return the same way back to the junction at Wp.6 (244M), where we turn right (E). The trail swings left then immediately, when a fainter branch continues straight on, right and descends to **Choza Chimoche** (Wp.17 245M). To the right of the shelter, a dirt road signed 'La

Caldera 2.9km' descends to the left of the big eucalyptus and the 'Limite Aprovechamiento Vecinal' sign. We follow the dirt road alongside an interesting *barranco* on our left hand side for 350 metres, where the dirt road swings left and a rather discreet trail continues straight ahead (Wp.18 250M). For a more relaxing stroll you can stay on the *pista*, but we take the shortcut, bearing right twice at junctions (both of the left branches connect with the dirt road visible from the junctions) to eventually meet the dirt road at a Y-junction of *pistas* (Wp.19 258M) at **Pasada de las Bestias**.

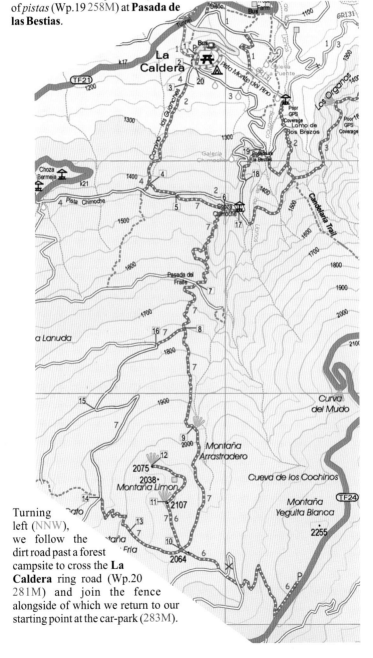

Turning left (NNW), we follow the dirt road past a forest campsite to cross the **La Caldera** ring road (Wp.20 281M) and join the fence alongside of which we return to our starting point at the car-park (283M).

8

High mountains mean big views and few routes come close to this combination of easy walking with magnificent views to be experienced on our **Arenas Negras** route from the **Visitors' Centre** at **El Portillo**. We climb 200-plus metres with not much happening in the first leg of the route, before it all comes; the views expand and expand, and if that isn't enough, the ground opens at our feet into a great chasm. Skitter down the side of a black sand cliff, and we have a terrific introduction to the excitements of **Las Cañadas**.

Mouflon restrictions: Due to mouflon control this route is <u>closed</u> when the restrictions are in place; see page 10 for details.

Access by bus: Nº342 from **Playa de las Américas** & **Los Cristianos**, Nº348 from **Puerto de la Cruz**; there's only one departure and return of these services each day, so make sure you don't miss your bus!

Access by car: Park at the **Visitors' Centre** car park at the start of our route, Km32.4 of the TF-21; usually plenty of spaces.

We start from the extensive parking area at the **Visitors' Centre** close to **El Portillo**. From the road we go past the mapboards and the vehicle barrier (Wp.1 0M) on the **Siete Cañadas** dirt *pista* (S) to cross a shallow valley before coming up to a signposted junction of *pistas* (Wp.2 5M) where we go left (trail **Nº2**) on the minor track.

Starting at Wp.1

It's a gentle ascent (ENE) in amongst the tundra, a soft landscape compared to much of **Las Cañadas**. When our *pista* swings right (Wp.3 13M) in a sharp U-bend, we bear left on a trail which takes us down to cross a ravine floor before climbing steadily up to pass a notice board on honey production in the National Park (Wp.4 17M).

Suitably informed, we resume our climb - surrounded by *retama* (white broom) shrubs, whose honey is so delicious and unique for its high altitude origin - to walk past a small barren slope (Wp.5 21M), where our trail's gradient eases. The surface turns from brown to grey, as we enjoy views below us, where the scenic TF-24 road crosses the high *cumbre* to **La Laguna** as views ahead open up over the **Orotava Valley** and **Puerto de la Cruz**, the **Los Realejos** *cumbre* looking particularly impressive from our elevated position.

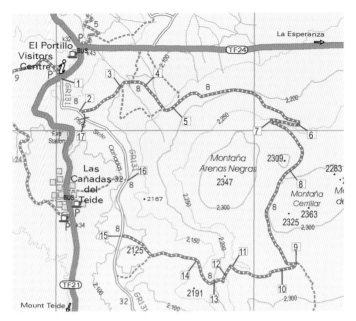

Our trail is climbing gently, almost contouring around **Montaña Arenas Negras** and bringing the **Izaña** observatory into view. We come across a short stretch of bare rock just before reaching a junction with trail **Nº37** in a hairpin bend (Wp.6 40M). Keeping right, we continue ascending through more broom to a second hairpin bend (Wp.7 45M) by large crumbly-looking rocks and a small cliff. More of the **Izaña** observatory comes into view as we traverse the lower slopes of **Montaña Arenas Negras**, gradually swinging south (S) as we climb.

Our route curves as we ascend between **Arenas Negras** and **Cerrillar** mountains, the climb gradually easing so that we are hardly aware of reaching the high point of our route as the magnificent panorama of **Mount Teide** comes into view (Wp.8 54M). Now we are back to easy strolling as our trail widens, allowing us to take in the panoramas as we progress. We gradually curve south-east, descending very gently to come to a junction (Wp.9 69M) on a plain, where the path ahead with a line of rocks across it is prohibited to access.

About to cross the colourful gully (Wp.10)

Turning right into the U-bend, we head exactly towards **Teide** (W) and come into a colourful gully (Wp.10 71M), which opens into a great chasm at our feet, as our trail leads us out of the gully and along the southern side of the canyon to bring the **Las Cañadas del Teide** restaurants into view (Wp.11 78M).

If the canyon was a surprise, we immediately come to another as our path takes us onto a black *picón* mountain, our route coming back to the canyon's edge before sweeping left across the steep black slope in a skittering descent to large rocks (Wp.12 82M).

Keeping left below the rocks, the trail is steeper as we zigzag down the black slopes as slowly as practical to keep a sure footing, before our trail runs off the slopes down onto a brown surface and into *retama* (Wp.13 86M), where it swings right (N) into a small gully and towards the canyon. Our route steepens for another skittery descent on *picón* before coming down over a couple of log steps to the floor of **Las Cañadas** (Wp.14 91M), the black mountain and giant canyon dominating the landscape behind us.

The valley floor makes for easy walking, as we head west along the left side of a valley, our route turning right in front of a hillock to eventually run out to meet the **Siete Cañadas** *pista* (Wp.15 103M).

Turning right (N) we stroll along the *pista*, which is pleasant enough, though nothing like as exciting as our earlier route. A short stiff ascent is dealt with before passing a path off to our left to **El Portillo Alto** (Wp.16 113M).

Between Wps.16 & 17

Easy strolling takes us past a vehicle barrier (Wp.17) before meeting our outward route at the *pista* junction (Wp.2 126M) and then up to the main road (131M).

You can savour this route a second time by driving up to the most southerly of the **Las Cañadas** restaurants, from whose terraces you have superb views across to that skittering black *picón* mountain descent, and the huge canyon that we nearly stepped into.

La Fortaleza's red cliffs provide one of Tenerife's classic high altitude walking routes. Views are spectacular from the peak of **La Fortaleza,** from the western end of the **La Fortaleza** massif, and from the **Riscos de La Fortaleza**, all of which are covered in this route. On a map the route looks straight forward, but the broken ground of **Las Cañadas** combined with the 2000+ metre altitude make it demanding, energy-sapping yet rewarding. We have moved our start to the **Visitor Centre** where we get the benefit of secure parking along with the centre's facilities while refreshments are down the road at **El Portillo** in the Bar/Rest close to the bus stop.

Mouflon restrictions: Due to mouflon control this route is <u>closed</u> when the restrictions are in place. See page 10 for details.

| 4 | 3½ H | 12.5 km | | 350m / 350m | out & back | 1* |

* None on the route though there's a Bar/Rest down the road at **El Portillo** by the bus stop.

Access by bus: Nº342 from **Playa de las Américas & Los Cristianos**, Nº348 from **Puerto de la Cruz,** to **El Portillo**; there's only one departure and return of these services each day, so make sure you don't miss your bus!

Access by car: Park at the **Visitor Centre El Portillo**, Km32.4 of the TF-21, offering plenty of space on either side of the road.

At the **Visitor Centre**, we go past the entrance gate (Wp.1 0M) to a mapboard at the start of our trail (National Park's routes **Nºs1** and **6**), just left of the main entrance of the **Centro de Visitantes** (Wp.2). Bearing left, we climb past the compound before descending to a trail junction (Wp.3 4M), where we turn left.

Wp.2, our trail left of the Visitor Centre entrance

Early stages of our route

The broad sandy trail takes us to a bowl where we snake between various rock formations to pass two stone benches at a junction (Wp.4 7M) where a stone-barred path forks off to the left. Keeping straight on, we climb out of the bowl to reach a crest at a smartly situated bench (Wp.5 13M) overlooking another depression. Down the trail we come onto a plain with a pine forest on our right. Coming past a faint fork to the right at a yellow 'El Portillo' arrow (Wp.6 18M), our trail swings left to come to a mapboard at a junction (Wp.7 19M) with trail **Nº6** to our left. We continue straight on before traversing a gentle slope to come to a junction (and a mapboard) with trail **Nº.24** to **El Portillo Alto** (Wp.8 24M), an alternative start for our **La Fortaleza** route.

We climb to the top of the crest past a big pyramid-like rock on the left of our trail before descending steadily through the broken land to pass a right-hand fork (Wp.9 31M) near the edge of the pine forest before climbing again. On past a weather station on our right, our route comes through a 'rock gateway' (Wp.10 42M), to head NW along several rock outcrops to reach the top of a slope overlooking the gravel plain below **La Fortaleza**, just after which we go straight on at the crossroads with trails **Nºs22** and **25** (Wp.11 49M).

Wp.12; Fortaleza in view

At the bottom of the rough path we come onto the plain (Wp.12) to head towards the start of a fenced area at a junction (Wp.13 56M). Both branches are part of our itinerary and first we bear right (trail **Nº29**) to the tree-dotted *degollada* with the shrine and to the top of **Fortaleza** for its magnificent views.

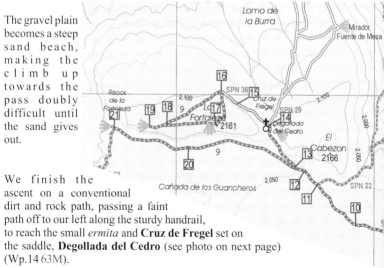

The gravel plain becomes a steep sand beach, making the climb up towards the pass doubly difficult until the sand gives out.

We finish the ascent on a conventional dirt and rock path, passing a faint path off to our left along the sturdy handrail, to reach the small *ermita* and **Cruz de Fregel** set on the saddle, **Degollada del Cedro** (see photo on next page) (Wp.14 63M).

From the *ermita* (0M), we take a dirt track north-west (joining official trail **Nº36**), which climbs gently past a small memorial shrine (Wp.15) before it finishes in open ground north of the **Fortaleza** peak (Wp.16 6M).

Clear trails go straight ahead (our return way) and to the left, which we take to steadily ascend (S) to the peak (Wp.17 14M) to emerge next to a big bush and a rock promontory to enjoy superb views.

From the summit a curved trail takes us westwards to pass between two pines, 50 metres after which we reach a signed Y-junction (Wp.18 21M).

Our return route is to the right, but we first go left for 200 metres to the dead-end signed *mirador* at a square of stones, the end of the official trail (Wp.19 24M). We walk back to Wp.18 to take the left branch and return to the *ermita* on the saddle (Wp.14) and then across the grit plain to the trail junction (Wp.13).

We turn right (WNW) joining the official trail below the cliffs of **La Fortaleza** and cross the wide sandy plain. Leaving the big fence behind, we join and shadow a smaller fence on our right before passing a small gate in it (Wp.20 16M), where the old rough trail from the *degollada* joins us. We continue out to a junction with trail **Nº33** at the **Riscos de la Fortaleza** (Wp.21 28M) for the impressive views out over the pine forest to the **Teno** mountains and the north-west coast of Tenerife.

It's time to head back to base, retracing our steps to the edge of the grit plain and taking the general trail across this strange phenomenon back to our entry point (Wp.12). A stiff climb up the eroded trail takes us back into the broken land of **Las Cañadas**. Again, this region of valleys, descents and ascents is tougher than it looks on the maps as we retrace our steps back to the **Visitor Centre**.

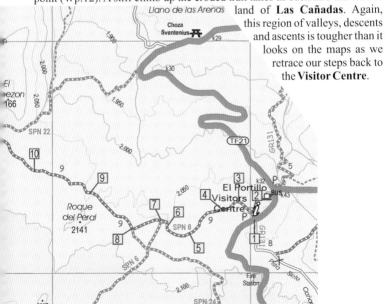

10

This walk follows one of the old donkey trails which link **Arona** and **Adeje**, although the old route has unfortunately been disrupted by high level developments in **Torviscas Alto**. For this eastern arm we have an easy country walk with impressive views, followed by our descent into the resort through the new developments to finish in **Torviscas** or **Fañabé**. Start with a relaxed ascent to **Arona** on the Titsa bus service.

The *camino rural* after Wp.5

Access by bus: N°s 480 & 482 link **Arona** with **Los Cristianos**.

We start from the **Arona** bus terminus (Wp.1 0M) on the

The sign at Wp.10

Avenida de la Constitución by strolling up the **Calle Duque de la Torre** paved street to the town square (Wp.2) and go left across the square to walk up the top road to cross the TF-51 onto the **Vento** road (Wp.3 8M), marked with a **GR131** waypost. Walking up the **Vento** road, we pass **Casa del Pintor** on our right before our route runs down to the **Obelisk** junction (Wp.4) in **Vento**.

Going left, we leave the **Roque del Conde/GR131** route of Walks 11 & 17 (Wp.5 18M) just before going left on a *camino rural* tarmac road. The narrow road drops down through abandoned terraces, passing an impressive house (Wp.6), before descending to a junction where another *camino rural* goes right across the *barranco* (Wp.7).

After a short uphill, houses line the road, then we drop steeply down to the TF-51 main road (Wp.8).

46

Watching out for traffic, we turn right to walk down the road past the Km3 marker to an old loop of the road (Wp.9) and on to the start of **Camino Viejo de Adeje** (Wp.10 38M) dirt road. The dirt road sweeps us down to cross the watercourse of the first *barranco* (Wp.11), prickly pear and *tabaiba* dotting the *malpaís*.

On the Camino Viejo de Adeje

We climb up to pass an abandoned house on our left (Wp.12) before the cobbled trail zigzags down to cross the **Barranco del Rey** (Wp.13).

A steady climb brings us up to meet the friendly dogs of a neat-walled farm (Wp.14 53M). Passing the farm on our left, we stroll across the gentle slopes towards a low ridge which ends in a rocky outcrop.

We pass a T-junction (Wp.15) where a dirt road goes right towards a white cottage, while we continue ahead on the water-eroded trail. The condition of the trail improves as we stroll up to meet a water channel on the ridge (Wp.16 60M) from where we have spectacular views down over a *caldera* to **Los Cristianos** and **Playa de las Américas**.

Alongside the water channel (Wp.16)

This ridge might seem quite insignificant when seen from the east, but we face a steep descent on its west side, zigzagging down a donkey trail. The loose stone surface makes for a slow, skittery descent until we cross a broad working water canal (Wp.17 69M) known locally as the **Río Conde**.

Now we are on the gentle dirt path which runs alongside the **Río Conde** to give us an easy stroll along to a dirt road junction (Wp.18) where we have the option to follow the **Río Conde** before finishing in **Fañabé** (see B at the end of text) or turn downhill to a second junction (Wp.19).

The main dirt road runs down to the water treatment works on the floor of the *caldera*, while we go right on a fainter grassy trail onto a saddle (Wp.20) between a water change point on the canal, and the **Picos las Américas** on our left, 80 metres before a ruined cottage (85M).

Looking in direction of Option A from Wp.20

Onward routes - there are two alternatives:

A
Go down into the development to follow the roads and/or staired pavements down to the entrance of **Balcones del Conde** (15-20M) and then down into the **Torviscas** region of **Las Américas**.

B
Go up to the **Río Conde**, easiest from the first dirt road junction (Wp.18) and follow the canal above the development to meet our Walk 12 'Adeje Skywalker', before descending on a dirt track to **Fañabé**.

Roque del Conde, seen from the Arona road

Roque del Conde's 1000 metre 'table top' peak dominates the coastal plain of southern Tenerife. The views from the top are simply stupendous, rewarding the stiff climb up this impressive mountain, which also appeals to plant enthusiasts.

This is a route for fit walkers, who can confidently tackle a climb totalling 450 metres on rough tracks requiring good, well cushioned, walking footwear.

4 | 3½ H | 11 km | 450m / 450m | out & back | 0

Access by car: Our starting point is at the junction of the **Vento** road with the TF-51, just above **Arona**'s town square, where there's plenty of parking; please do not park on the narrow roads in **Vento** village.

Access by bus: Bus N°s 480 & 482 take you from **Playa de las Américas/Los Cristianos** to the **Arona** terminus. Walk up the street to the town square to take the **Calle San Carlos Borromeo** from the north-west corner of the square. Climb up the steep street, then cross carefully over the main road to start point by the **GR131** waypost.

From the 'GR131' waypost (Wp.1 0M), we climb up from the main road to views down to the coast as the lane swings left and past **La Casa del Pintor** *casa rural* before the lane runs down between the first houses of **Vento**.

We stroll down to the religious obelisk at a T-junction (Wp.2 6M) and turning left we come down to the **Roque del Conde/GR131** path (Wp.3) which is signed off to our right by house N°78. A wall plaque over a green painted shutter immediately after we've turned right informs us that this house was built in 1852.

Green shutters and wall plaque after Wp.3

After the tarmac we are on a well-made *sendero* which drops us down into the **Barranco de las Casas** (Wp.4). Our trail runs up over rock to a crest and then drops us down into the **Barranco del Ancón** (Wp.5). Across the valley floor, a gentle climb brings us up alongside the *barranco* where the **GR131** goes right

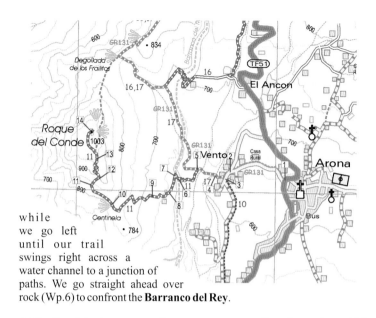

while
we go left
until our trail
swings right across a
water channel to a junction of
paths. We go straight ahead over
rock (Wp.6) to confront the **Barranco del Rey**.

At the lip of the *barranco* wall we come onto a well-made *sendero* which zigzags steeply down towards the ravine floor. Stone walls with posts mounted in them line the *sendero*, as we drop down on its rough boulder surface. After twists and turns we come onto the valley floor, with sheer cliff walls rising fifty metres up on each side of us.

Straight across the valley floor, we come onto another rough boulder *sendero* to start climbing. We toil up the stiff climb until a set of stone steps brings us up to the top of the *barranco* wall (Wp.7). Ahead, **Roque del Conde** looms over us as we take a path to our left. Climbing up past a white arrow, our dirt path winds its way up to a gold rock slab, with views back to **Vento**, and continues on towards a crumbling cottage.

Over a small crest the path runs down past a small water cistern the size of a bath, on our right (Wp.8 28M). Above the water cistern, unseen by most walkers, is an opening in the rock. Climbing up the rock slope, we find ourselves looking through the narrow opening into a large subterranean cavern. A small channel, now mostly silted up, guides water into the cavern. In the far distant past, long before pipes and water channels, this substantial cistern was the main water storage in this area. You can get an idea of the cavern's size by shouting into it and waiting for the echo! Leaving this historical site we drop back down onto the path to continue on to the cottage.

Our trail climbs up past the north wall of the cottage. We pass two threshing circles on our left as we continue up over the abandoned terraces to come onto a boulder-laid donkey trail (Wp.9) to continue straight uphill. Our trail swings left for us to head diagonally across the slope in a relentless climb towards the saddle at **Centinela**. At the end of the 'long straight', the donkey trail becomes rougher and continues upwards through a series of zigzags as we climb towards the saddle. It's a steep, relentless climb, so pace yourself and take rests whenever necessary. We come onto another 'long straight' of the donkey trail and continue toiling upwards. The donkey trail swings right for yet another 'long straight' pointing towards **Roque del Conde**, before swinging left for the last 'long straight' of the route. At the end of the last 'long straight' we swing right and the donkey trail finishes for us to continue climbing on a narrow dirt trail. We climb steeply up through a series of zigzags to reach the saddle at **Centinela** (Wp.10 51M). Our trail opens out into a small clear area, forming an unofficial *mirador*; spectacular views open up over the resorts 700 metres below us.

From **Centinela** a narrow trail goes right (NW) along the ridge towards **Roque del Conde**. Our route undulates along to take us across the southern face of the mountain until we swing right (Wp.11) for a zigzag ascent. We come above the hidden valley which lies behind **Playa de las Américas**, the head of the valley and one ridge filled with *embalses* while the floor is covered with banana plantations. The loose rock and dirt trail climbs steeply to bring us up onto sheets of orange rock below ten metre high cliffs (Wp.12).

On the peak

Going left, we continue to circle the mountain following the trail as it climbs around rock promontories. It's onwards and upwards through a series of steep climbs, the path splitting and rejoining just above a 'TS4' white paint marker.

Asphodels on the peak

A final toiling ascent brings us onto the edge of the plateau (Wp.13 83M), and a surprise. On the mountain-top we find long abandoned agricultural terraces - sometime in the distant past someone used to farm this least accessible area of land!

A path, trodden down by walkers, leads across the terraces towards the mound and height marker at the official peak of **Roque del Conde**. As we approach the peak we find the large mound covered in a sea of asphodels (Asphodelus tenuifolius), a beautiful sight when in flower from February to May.

Pushing through the flowers, we come to the height marker (Wp.14 88M). **Roque del Conde** is the final mountain in the chain surrounding **Las Cañadas**, and inland is the 'turret' peak of **Roque Imoque**. From here, standing suspended high above the surrounding lands, we have awesome views over the south and west coasts - a fitting reward for our efforts.

There is an 'experts only' route down the north face of **Conde** which joins Walks 16 & 17 at the **Degollada de los Frailitos**, for the adventurous seeking a circular route taking in **Roque del Conde**.

We return by the same route taking care on the steep descent down to the *mirador*, after which the path and donkey trail make for an easier descent, though it can be hard on the knees. The climbs out of the three *barrancos*, particularly **Barranco del Rey**, give us a reminder of our earlier efforts before we arrive back at **Arona**.

Breathtaking views north from the peak

'Skywalker' refers to the elevated views, giving the impression of being suspended above the southern landscapes - but it comes at a price. While most of our route involves easy walking on a paved water canal, the **Río Conde**, we face a stiff ascent to the canal and then have to cross an extremely vertiginous aqueduct (though it can by avoided by climbing down through the ravine bed; use of hands and buttocks needed!) and edge around a mountain above sheer drops; a good head for heights and sure-footedness are essential. There are also some sections where the paving is cracked or missing, requiring care. There's the option of a visit to **The White House** before finally heading down to **Playa de las Américas**.

*** Easy stroll**: As an alternative to our 'expert' start from **Adeje** to the aqueduct, new development means that we can now drive up to the **Río Conde** canal on the highest **Torviscas Alto** developments, offering the option for an easy stroll along the paved canal to southern Tenerife's very own **White House**; see the walk description at the end of the main route description.

Access by bus: Adeje is a 'county' town with good bus services. Routes Nºs 417, 447, 460 & 473 link **Los Cristianos/Playa de las Américas** with **Adeje**.

We start out from the bus stop by the top end of **Adeje** *cementerio* (cemetery), to go right in a few steps onto a dirt road (Wp.1 0M), immediately passing a barrier with a dubious 'Authorized personnel only' sign. Our dirt road winds down into the *barranco* to cross the watercourse (Wp.2), coming to a dirt cross roads where we go straight over to walk up the higher dirt road, which narrows to a track and becomes rougher as we climb up onto the ridge at a U-bend with palms.

The cottage between Wps.2 & 3

Now the dirt track heads up the line of the ridge, passing a white cottage on our right and coming up to a junction just past a water tank (Wp.3 20M).

Water pipes cross our route as we continue left on the dirt track towards the mountains.

As we gain height and the track becomes rougher, we pass an 'Espacio Natural Protegido Barranco del Infierno' sign, 50 metres after which we take the cairn-marked path to the right (Wp.4 29M) before bearing right again one minute later, then left 30 metres after, where the path straight on is barred by stones (Wp.5).

Just a few more steps and we finally clamber up onto the canal (Wp.6).

We're on a paved metre wide water canal. It's an easy walking surface except for the wobbly and missing slabs, so take care to 'look where you walk, and STOP to look at the views', as there is no protection from the drops alongside the canal.

An easy stroll takes us over a small bridge (Wp.7) before we curve round into a smaller *barranco* to cross its watercourse on another bridge (Wp.8 50M), then step out to a viewpoint (Wp.9). As the canal turns into the next *barranco* it becomes vertiginous, with sheer drops on our right and a cliff on our left.

Vertiginous cliff section (Wps.9-10), the aqueduct in view

The aqueduct (Wp.10)

If you have any doubts over this section, return towards **Adeje**. We approach the major obstacle on our route, an aqueduct (Wp.10) which carries the canal over the steep **Barranco del Agua** dropping down from **Roque Abinque**.

In this dramatic orogenic setting of soaring mountains, cliffs and sheer *barrancos*, we edge over the ten metre span to its eastern end (60M). In case of even light winds climb down through the ravine and back up to the canal rather than attempt the aqueduct. We soon face another vertiginous section where the canal runs under a cliff and there are some missing slabs; here we step onto the black water pipe to carefully negotiate these sections. Turning out of the main **Barranco del Agua** ravine, we cross a small bridge (Wp.11) to enter a landscape of gentler slopes. After another bridge (Wp.12) we walk out to a *mirador* view (Wp.13 78M) as the **Río Conde** swings left. A steel water pipe crosses the canal just before we cross the **Morro Grueso** ridge (Wp.14) to swing above the **Fañabé** valley. Curving left we see the **Río Conde** sweeping around the broad valley ahead of us.

Easy strolling takes us past a small cave and over a small bridge (Wp.15 98M), before we come to a section where rocks and earth cover the canal (Wp.16). Picking our way over the rock, we come back onto the paved canal to pass a dirt road on our right and cross a small bridge (Wp.17) before coming to a water change point (Wp.18 110M) where we drop down onto a dirt road which runs alongside the canal. We follow the dirt road until it swings right to drop into the valley where we clamber back onto the paved canal.

After crossing a bridge and a small canal which crosses the **Río Conde**, we come to a difficult water change point (Wp.19).

Some nimble footwork is needed to negotiate the inland scrub and change point to get back onto the paved canal. We stroll on, the dirt road alongside the canal turning away towards an abandoned cottage on the saddle between two valleys, then we climb over a small rock slip (Wp.20), taking care where there are occasional missing slabs before we're below **The White House** which sits above water change points numbered 195-9 and 194-8 (Wp.21 124M). In a couple of minutes the canal passes underground and is crossed by means of the rough dirt access track to **The White House** (Wp.22) which gives us the choice of an uphill diversion to one of the region's most noticeable but least visited landmarks - see the *'Easy Stroll Alternative for Car Drivers'* at the end of this walk description.

Now we leave the **Río Conde** to head down the rough dirt track past a large water

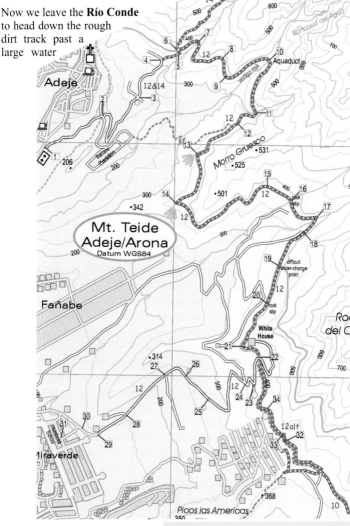

tank on our left (Wp.23), to a junction of dirt tracks (Wp.24 140M). Our dirt track is littered with shale and scree, making for slow skittery progress down past water tanks; those to the left (Wp.25) old and empty, and new and fenced to the right (Wp.26), before the track heads straight down the side of the valley. Our walking surface improves as we pass dirt tracks, to the left (Wp.27) and on the right (Wp.28), before we reach the first house and a tarmac lane (Wp.29 165M) to stroll down past the impressive entrance to **Finca Amapola de Fañabé** (Wp.30), then come onto the new road system behind the **Humboldt School** (Wp.31 170M). We make our way to alongside the motorway with the pedestrian bridge giving us access to **Fañabé**'s streets.

An alternative finish involves continuing on the **Río Conde** to the new developments and then heading ('Down to Town') down to **Torviscas Alto** and on down into the main resort area.

* Easy Stroll Alternative for car drivers from **Torviscas Alto** to **The White House**

From the **Torviscas/Playa Fañabé** motorway junction head inland up past **Villa Tagoro** on **Calle Galicia** to drive through the impressive arched entrance into the 'Roque del Conde' developments, still on **Calle Galicia**. Negotiate your way up, turning left at **Supermarket El Conde**, to the highest cul-de-sac to park (Wp.32) just below the saddle that features in Walk 10 'Down to Town'.

A clear path climbs up towards a gurgling water point on the canal, then levels out below the **Río Conde** to a viaduct over a water run off (Wp.33 5M) where we face a scrambling ascent alongside a water pipe to cross the canal onto a path that takes us over the run off on a wooden bridge before coming back to the canal. At a water point (Wp.34), there's a small diversion before concrete stairs take us back to the canal path, passing two more water points; the path is little walked and surprisingly floriferous making secateurs useful.

As **The White House** looms over us, the path takes us down to join its access track (Wp.22 24M).

We turn up the access track to cross the **Río Conde** for a steady ascent up the rough jeep track, getting rougher as it heads away from our objective before swinging back for us to trudge up to **The White House** (36M).

Our objective; The White House

After enjoying the elevated views from the pumping station, you could opt to continue along the **Río Conde**, easy walking until you approach the aqueduct, enjoying this unusual perspective of the resort areas along the coast. Otherwise, we return by retracing our route.

This is an easy route on old donkey trails taking in spectacular views, with excellent flora including an unusual floral phenomenon. After a rather unpromising start the landscape exudes bucolic charm; in short, it's idyllic walking country and with a classic *típico*, **Bar Taucho**, not far away.

Access by car: We start by driving west on the TF-1 motorway past **Adeje** and onto the TF-82 to look for a right turning (easily missed) onto the TF-583 road to **Taucho**. After the twisting low gear ascent, follow the narrow road through **Taucho** (past **Bar Taucho**) to continue on the narrow lane as it drops into and climbs out of a *barranco* until we come to **La Quinta** church on our left and a parking area.

Wp.1 at the church square

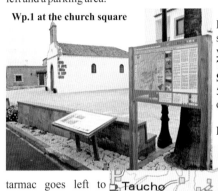

From the corner of the church square (Wp.1 0M) we take the yellow/white marked **PR TF 71.1** to stroll along **Calle La Serrería** before leaving it in 55 metres to go right (Wp.2) onto a smaller tarmac lane.

Down into a small valley, the tarmac goes left to houses as we step right onto a broad dirt road (Wp.3) for 70 metres before bearing right onto a waymarked trail to continue below and along electricity lines. Our trail descends across a slope of agave and crosses bare rock to join an old concrete canal before crossing a watercourse.

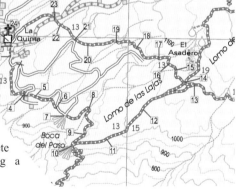

We come up to cross a dirt road 10 metres from a rusty gate (Wp.4) to clamber up over rock following the donkey trail as it skirts a fenced area, passing gates and an *embalse* (Wp.5), to come onto another dirt road. Crossing a doubled canal, we shortly take the track parallel to the dirt road alongside a small *barranco*, which narrows to a trail and soon curves right to cross its floor, then brings us onto the dirt road arriving from our left (Wp.6). We swing along to a *parapente* launch point (Wp.7), with an unusual official sign, to continue on a walking trail dropping into a steeper *barranco*. Across the watercourse

Wp.10

(Wp.8), we climb up the southern wall, crossing a side *barranco* (Wp.9) for a final ascent to **Boca del Paso**, the head of **Lomo de las Lajas** ridge (Wp.10 28M), with its

Carved canal after Wp.12

impressive views to the south over **Adeje** and the coast. Leaving **Boca del Paso**, we go east to pick up the eroded walking trail which climbs steadily and curves left (part of our 'Queen Of The South' route in reverse). Our eroded trail brings us up to a gentle open ridge (Wp.11) ahead of us, then a path takes us up the left side of the ridge in a steady climb, crossing a rock section (Wp.12).

Continuing our steady climb, the path splits (the left branch goes directly to Wp.14) as we keep right to come amongst the pines on a well defined path to reach a junction (Wp.13 47M) where we go left, leaving our 'Queen Of The South' route, passing a large green dot to climb up to a crossroads with the **Camino de Teresme** route (our 'Las Lajas - Adeje' walk) on the crest of the ridge (Wp.14) with its carved water channels. Waymarks guide us (NW) on a faint path which zigzags down to the floor of the small valley (Wp.15), below an old cottage, then gently climbs up to cross a small ridge where we meet a steel water pipe (Wp.16).

Now we follow the pipe steeply down into an unusual *barranco*, its floor completely choked with brambles which stretch as far as we can see in a great green swathe. We zigzag down before following the southern side to cross the watercourse (Wp.17 58M), at a cutting through the brambles, before climbing up over an old water canal to ascend the northern side still accompanied by the pipe. As we climb and move away from the valley, the bramble-choked watercourse is even more impressive until we turn away (Wp.18) to drop into another valley to cross its watercourse just below a mature pine (Wp.19), before a steady climb up for our path to cross open ground (Wp.20).

There are houses ahead of us as we descend alongside the pipe into another small valley (Wp.21) and climb up the path to cross open ground and into a minor valley (Wp.22) before climbing up the rough stone trail between stone walls to reach a tarmac lane (Wp.23) opposite house Nº21.

Across the lane, the water pipe continues past the fence of house Nº21 with its noisy dog. The trail swings left (SW) 40 metres off the lane to continue alongside electricity poles. Five minutes later a trail with a new handrail feeds in from our right (Wp.24), seventy metres away from our starting point by the church (83M).

58

Our 'Wow! Spectacular' route follows the **Camino Carrasco** donkey trail linking **Ifonche** with **Adeje**. As it requires us to complete 3.2kms road walking from the TF-51 to **Ifonche** before we pick up the *camino*, it's best walked late morning when the two bars (open at 10am) and **Bar/Rest El Dornajo** (**Ifonche**, open 12ish) can provide outward refreshments.

From **Ifonche** we have the most exciting mountain descent in the south of Tenerife, but at the price of it being a tricky, picky trail, vertiginous in places, only suitable for experienced walkers in good weather. All the most challenging parts of the trail come shortly after leaving **Ifonche** (Wp.9), so you can use this as your decision point for whether to continue on the full route, or to backtrack (to Wp.6) to follow our straightforward 'Queen of the South' route down to **Adeje**. The mountain scenery and views are magnificent, so if you have the ability and good weather, this is your route.

* if walked later in the day, there are three bars likely to be open on the first section, plus choices in **Adeje** at any time.

Access by bus: Nº342 from **Playa de las Américas** and **Los Cristianos**, or Nº482 from **Los Cristianos**. Ask for **Cruce de Ifonche**, which is 350 metres after **Café Altavista/Casa Camilo**; the **La Escalona** stop is a few hundred metres further up the TF-51.

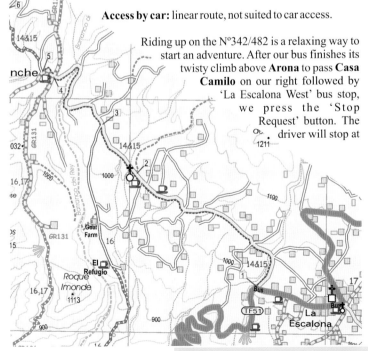

Access by car: linear route, not suited to car access.

Riding up on the Nº342/482 is a relaxing way to start an adventure. After our bus finishes its twisty climb above **Arona** to pass **Casa Camilo** on our right followed by 'La Escalona West' bus stop, we press the 'Stop Request' button. The driver will stop at

Cruce de Ifonche junction (Wp.1 0M) for us to alight. We set off up the **Ifonche** TF-567 road (N) to swing over the *barranco*'s stone bridge for a second climb up to a crest of the road, giving views over the plateau ahead.

As the narrow road sweeps down we have an easy stroll across the landscape dotted with *fincas* while ahead, the peaks of **Imoque** and **Brezos** mark the plateau's southern limits.

El Dornajo (Wp.4)

... towards an isolated cottage ... (near Wp.6)

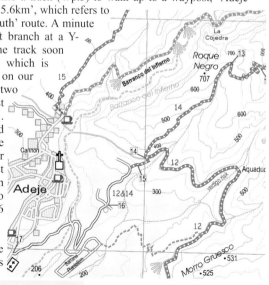

Past **Bar/Rest Hermano Pedro**, then **Bar Tasca Taguara**, we come to the lonely *ermita* (Wp.2 20M) with a potable water tap and a dirt track signed for **Vilaflor**. Next is the **El Refugio** track to our left (Wp.3 27M) and we're now sharing the road with our 'Fantasia' route.

After undulating across the plateau, our road drops into the **Barranco del Rey** followed by a steep climb up to the tarmac crossroads at **Bar/Rest El Dornajo** (Wp.4 41M) in **Ifonche**.

Straight over the crossroads, we continue on the tarmac lane for 120 metres before turning right onto a track (Wp.5) to walk up to a waypost, 'Adeje 9.8km/Boca del Paso 5.6km', which refers to our 'Queen of the South' route. A minute later we take the left branch at a Y-junction of tracks, the track soon dwindling to a trail, which is shadowed by a canal on our left to wind through two small valleys amongst pine-dotted slopes. Coming over a red earth spur, where we cross a dirt track, our trail drops down past old terraces towards an isolated cottage to meet a dirt track (Wp.6 57M).

Here 'Queen of the South' continues

Deep, isn't it? Barranco del Infierno

ahead, while we go left, signed 'La Vista' on a stone, toward a power pole to walk up past **Casa Benítez** to a large threshing circle enjoying a *mirador* viewpoint of **La**

Vista above the **Barranco del Infierno** - deep, isn't it? From the threshing circle we ignore a left branch to continue along the track for 200 metres, taking a path to our right which immediately comes to the lip of the *barranco* (Wp.7 64M), where one path goes straight sticking to the ridge line, but we bear slightly to the right onto the descending path by a faint 'Reserva Natural' sign; we're now on the **Camino Carrasco**.

On the narrow ledge after Wp.7

Our stone-laid donkey trail drops steeply down the *barranco* wall into an amazing pocket of flora. Here on a narrow ledge running under sheer cliffs, and watered by the trade winds driven up the ravine, are some of the best examples of Tenerife's endemic plant life. It's a narrow path requiring careful footwork at times as we pass below the cliffs before ascending onto a saddle of sand-gold rock (Wp.8 82M) between

The sand-gold saddle (Wp.8)

the cliff outcrop and **Roque Abinque**.

From the east side of the saddle we take a small cairned path running along above the **Barranco del Agua**, ahead **Playa de las Américas** is framed by the *barranco* walls, and a rock 'finger' indicates our next destination. At a junction 40 metres after the saddle, we keep left, the path right heading up **Roque Abinque**. Our path is coming above an old water canal which we drop down to meet while running out towards the 'finger'. We now follow the canal, an eroded section requiring us to edge along the canal itself, to bring us to a right turn beside the 'rock football' topped 'finger' (Wp.9 95M) where a section of the old canal provides a gallery seat for us to look down through the orogenical landscape onto **Adeje**.

On the next section the path has fallen away! This means that we must cross a section of the narrow old canal where a protruding rock threatens to tip you over the abyss, admittedly not an extreme drop, but still a drop to trigger the vertigo. ("I got across so it can't be that bad!" (David)). This is quite the worst hazard on the **Camino Carrasco**, sections after this are merely 'tricky', and we'll understand if you turn back at this point; not that your day is lost because you have the choice of returning to 'Queen of the South' for the conventional descent to **Adeje**, or back to **El Dornajo** for 'Fantasia' with the option to finish in **Arona**, both with regular bus services.

Across the vertiginous canal section, our narrow trail now twists steeply down into the *barranco*, to pass under cliffs and striations of orange rock on a picky descent due to loose rock on the trail, to 'red rock' corner (Wp.10) with a panorama overlooking **Adeje** and the **Río Conde**'s aqueduct experienced on 'Adeje Skywalker'. On the next section we have a couple of landslips that require careful edging across, that's in addition to the loose rocks on the trail and intrusive shrubbery before we arrive at 'candelabra spurge' corner (Wp.11 120M) with its seat-like rocks.

Now we're amongst steep slopes rather than the sheer cliffs of earlier, with a stone laid trail to zigzag down over a ridge, bringing **Adeje** and the **Río Conde** back into view. At another natural *mirador* (Wp.12 140M) we take a break; it's a long way down requiring concentration on the rock-littered trail, so best to take breaks following our maxim of 'Stop to look at the view, and look where you're walking'.

We continue down the stone-littered, picky descent with its intrusive shrubs, until a small ascent takes us into a side valley, our trail running along to cross the watercourse (Wp.13) before we turn back towards **Adeje**. If anything the rock litter gets worse, requiring concentration for every step, as we slowly edge downwards to come onto the **Río Conde** canal (Wp.14).

Taking the **Adeje** path on the other side of the canal, we are on another picky descent to a jeep track (Wp.15), a junction easily missed if walked as an ascent. The jeep track is little better than the path, somewhat alleviated by the lush endemic plant life, until we come onto a dirt track (Wp.16) by a square *embalse* and at last we have a decent walking surface on which to head down into the *barranco*. Bearing straight on at crossroads, a final uphill slog brings us up to the road alongside the cemetery (Wp.17 225M).

The nearest bus stop is downhill opposite the sports centre, while the closest refreshments are a hundred metres uphill, towards the town centre.

This walk certainly lives up to its royal title. We start at the **Ifonche** junction and set out on a journey through a 'timescape' of agricultural settlements, pine forests, incredible *barrancos* and valleys, to emerge at the best *mirador* view in the south. The final descent of 650 metres altitude into **Adeje** is unfortunately more memorable for the rough trail than the views - good footwear is essential - but don't let this put you off this grand walk.

4 | 4H | 14 km | 250m / 900m | one way | 4*

* El Dornajo in Ifonche, Otelo in Adeje

Alternative start

An alternative but tougher start can be made from **Arona**, by either walking up the **Vilaflor** road to the **Granja Arona** where we take the track down to the embalse in 'Fantasia' (Walk 16) to follow its return route to **Ifonche**, or take the **GR131** (Walk 17) in reverse from **Arona** through **Vento** to **Ifonche**, much more scenic but tougher and longer.

Access by bus: Nº342 from **Playa de las Américas/Los Cristianos**, Nº482 from **Los Cristianos**. Ask for **Cruce de Ifonche**; this bus stop is 350 metres after **Café Altavista/Casa Camilo** restaurant seen on the right; some visitors call this stop 'La Escalona' but that is further up the TF-51.

Access by car: linear route not suited to car access.

From the bus stop at **Cruce de Ifonche** (Wp.1 0M) we follow our 'Wow! Spectacular to Adeje' start description (Wps.1, 2, 3, 4, 5 & 6 same for both routes) to arrive at **Bar/Rest El Dornajo** (Wp.4 41M). Along the common route we take the track (Wp.5) to the right, then the left branch at Y-junction, which narrows down to a trail to come down to head straight across the dirt road in the bottom

Near the start after El Dornajo

of the valley (Wp.6 57M).

Our narrow walking trail climbs up from the valley floor and turns inland to steadily ascend the ridge, bringing us up to a bowl of old terraces

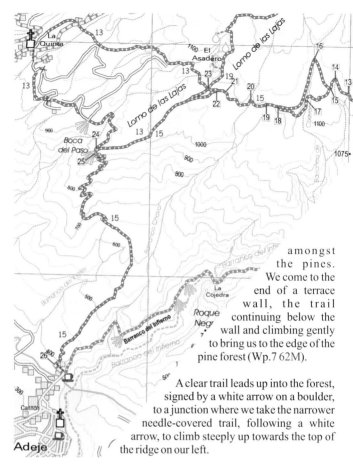

amongst the pines. We come to the end of a terrace wall, the trail continuing below the wall and climbing gently to bring us to the edge of the pine forest (Wp.7 62M).

A clear trail leads up into the forest, signed by a white arrow on a boulder, to a junction where we take the narrower needle-covered trail, following a white arrow, to climb steeply up towards the top of the ridge on our left.

White arrow waymarks keep us on the trail as we climb through a series of bends (Wp.8) to the crest of the ridge. On the ridge, large arrows made of rocks point in both directions along the trail; a small cairn marks the continuation of our trail and we go gently downhill. On our left is the **Barranco del Infierno** as our trail runs downhill, with occasional climbs, along the wall of this magnificent canyon. We walk below sheer cliffs, the long drop into the canyon on our left, as we progress towards the head of the *barranco*. The pine needle-covered path drops steeply, requiring care on the slippery surface, before levelling out to run below an impressive promontory.

Sounds of running water and the waterfall come up from the canyon's depths, and passing through a rock channel, we go downhill to round a pocket in the canyon wall. The trail runs down and out of the pocket to round a promontory by a mature Canarian pine; from here we enjoy *mirador* views down into the sheer-sided *barranco*. After the viewing point we come to a trail junction (Wp.9 73M). We take the right hand path to climb steeply up the narrow trail along the *barranco* wall. The path zigzags up to come under cliffs as we continue through a rock channel, and then more cliffs before the ascent eases.

We now stroll along to an area where the tumbled boulders of a huge rock slide cover the steep slopes. Our trail cuts through the sea of boulders to drop steeply down until we come out onto the floor of the canyon (Wp.10 83M), now above the **Barranco del Infierno** and technically on the floor of **Barranco de la Fuente**.

Picking our way over the grey boulders, we start climbing up the western wall of the canyon. It's a stiff ascent on the steep rocky trail, increasingly pine needle-covered as we climb before the path levels out and we come under a large boulder. Our route undulates along the *barranco* wall before taking another climb. Pacing ourselves for the stiff ascent and taking rests when necessary, we toil up to come above the canyon (Wp.11). Looking back across the *barranco* we can see that we've climbed back up to a similar altitude to the trail's start at **Ifonche**.

After the exertions of climbing out of the **Barranco de la Fuente** our trail leaves the views behind and takes us into a rather sombre section of pine forest which clothes a land of valleys and rugged *barrancos*.

Our trail is clearly waymarked, as we cross gentle valleys (Wp.12) and two sharp-sided *barrancos* (Wps.13 & 14) beneath the shade of the silent forest. A few cistus 'rock rose' bushes are relieving the tedium of this brown needle-covered ground. As the valleys become shallower we need to pay careful attention to the route's waymarking.

Coming up a gentle slope we approach a pair of pines where the main path turns right (Wp.15 101M); looking to our right we see an arrow twenty metres up the gentle slope. Although this appears to be a major junction, both paths arrive at the same destination, the right hand path crossing **Barranco Chavon** at Wp.16 while the straight-on path crosses it at Wp.17 then, after climbing out of the *barranco*, runs on through the pines to a path junction (Wp.18 117M) where we join the upper crossing route.

Now the forest becomes more colourful as the trail leads us through a series of shallow valleys (Wps.19, 20 & 21) to a junction at the edge of the forest (Wp.22 133M). Ahead, the main trail leads up onto an area of clear rock where there is an important wayposted crossroads with 'Camino de Teresme' (Wp.23 134M), where the main route to **La**

The crossroads at Wp.23

Quinta/Taucho continues straight ahead.

Views from Lomo de las Lajas

Views from Lomo de las Lajas

Following the left hand trail for 'Adeje/Boca del Paso', we come onto bare rock to find a hand-carved rock water channel. Boots have worn faint trails across the rock for us to parallel the small water channel. Away on our right we look over a *barranco* to the outlying houses of **Taucho** village, as our path continues

Boca del Paso (Wp.25)

going gently downhill to an area of red earth marked by a cairn. This path swings right to run along below a low ridge and becomes badly water-eroded before it meets a path from **La Quinta** (Wp.24) and then swings left onto the donkey trail at **Boca del Paso** (Wp.25 152M) with its superb panoramic views.

The descent from **Boca del Paso** at the end of the **Lomo de las Lajas** ridge starts well on a stone-laid donkey trail descending below orange cliffs. However, at the end of this short section the trail deteriorates into a rocky, boulder strewn, path which has suffered severe water erosion.

It's a long, tortuous, winding route down the mountainside requiring continuous concentration on what might be the roughest trail on the island - well cushioned footwear is absolutely essential. Having to concentrate on every footfall doesn't allow much opportunity to look at the scenery, and makes the last hour of the walk seem even longer.

Eventually our downward toil finishes when we meet the concrete (Wp.26) and stroll down the smooth surface to the start of the **Barranco del Infierno** walk (242M) at **Otelo**'s restaurant (open daily). We continue down the steep lane into **Adeje** for refreshment, and buses back to the resorts.

To find bus stops in **Adeje** follow **Calle de los Molinos** past **Bar Otelo** down for 300 metres to **Casa Fuerte** (fort). To reach the bus stop for the Nºs 447 & 448, carry straight on (**Calle Castillo**) for another 300 metres. For the Nºs 417, 460 and 473 buses, turn left at **Casa Fuerte** and continue past the church and *ayuntamiento* on **Calle Grande** to find bus stops at **Plaza Venezuela** (*Centro de Salud*).

When we pioneered this spectacular route on its (then) little-known trails we never imagined that it would be made 'official'. But even the authorities know a good thing when they see it, so the section from **Ifonche** to the edge of **Barranco del Rey** is now the **GR131**; see Walk 17. Whether it's mountains, spectacular views, a hidden valley, verdant plant life or unusual geology which you find most breathtaking, the sum of these parts is pure 'Fantasia' - truly one of the south's most interesting routes.

Access by bus: We start by catching the Nº342 or Nº482 bus up to the **Ifonche** junction (**Cruce de Ifonche**) bus stop to follow the 'Wow! Spectacular to Adeje' and 'Queen of the South' routes along the road to **Bar/Rest El Dornajo** (Wp.17 3.2km) in **Ifonche**. (If you can get a lift or taxi to **Ifonche** you can reduce your walking time by three quarters of an hour.)

At **El Dornajo** we turn left (S) to walk along the narrow road, passing another tiny road going up to the left while we continue straight on. On our right is a farm, its massive terrace walls giving the look of a fortified promontory. After running downhill the road climbs up to a house before levelling out to run along to a road junction with a sturdy wooden cross set in a concrete base (Wp.1 4km) where a road drops down into the valley on our left.

Access by car: Follow the same directions as for bus travellers and park near the wooden cross; parking at **El Dornajo** is often rather fraught.

From the cross (Wp.1 0M), we stroll along the lane heading for **Roque Imoque** passing **García's Nose** and **Roque de los Brezos**. Our lane descends gently through Canarian pines as we walk above abandoned terraces on our left, undulating along below **Roque de los Brezos** to come above cultivated terraces and a farm house. Ahead is the saddle between the *roques* of **Imoque** and **Brezos** which is our first destination; marked by a **GR131** waypost.

As the road swings left towards the farmhouse, we look for a path (Wp.2 8M) which runs below the ridge to cross the open ground and climb gently up to the saddle. If you miss the first path, look for the official **GR131** trail further down towards the farmhouse. *N.B.* Do not go past the farmhouse on the lane as its backyard is filled with hunting dogs and a couple of guard dogs!

Reaching the saddle a large *era* (threshing circle) (Wp.3) provides a spectacular view down over **Las Américas**. From the saddle, it's worth making a detour to the right to the peak of **Roque de los Brezos**

The *era* and views (Wp.3) as seen on the detour

along a good path for great views (not counted in our timing). We stroll over to the **GR131** waypost to take the official trail down the west side of **Imoque**. It is a narrow, trenched, stone-littered trail making for a picky descent before a small ascent brings us up onto the top of a spur to overlook the gentle landscape of the 'hidden valley' (Wp.4). Neat, though abandoned terraces ring this bowl in the mountains, where in spring field marigolds create a golden carpet, adding to the atmosphere.

Our **GR131** trail runs down the promontory passing below an *era* (Wp.5 40M), set on the saddle between the rounded hills after which a steep rock descent drops us down to pass an area of shattered rock after which our route is easier as it takes us onto a trail junction on the **Degollada de los Frailitos** saddle between **Imoque** and **Conde** (Wp.6 55M). Straight ahead, a trail leads to the northern ascent/descent of **Roque del Conde** while the **GR131** turns left (SE) to head down a shallow valley.

After the steep, picky, descent to the *degollada*, we drop down to follow a watercourse running along the valley floor (SE).

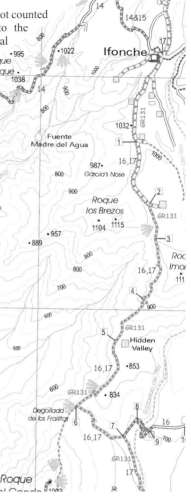

Looking back on our route

The great bulk of **Roque del Conde** looms over us on our right as we have an easy stroll down to a trail junction (Wp.7) marked by a 'GR131' waypost. Here the **GR131** heads south to meet the **Roque del Conde** trail before crossing the *barrancos* into **Vento**.

Where the **GR131** goes right, we continue straight ahead on the (now) minor trail which brings us to the lip of the **Barranco del Rey** and along to the top of

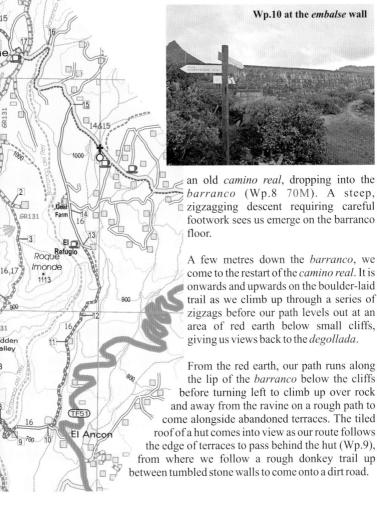

Wp.10 at the *embalse* wall

an old *camino real*, dropping into the *barranco* (Wp.8 70M). A steep, zigzagging descent requiring careful footwork sees us emerge on the barranco floor.

A few metres down the *barranco*, we come to the restart of the *camino real*. It is onwards and upwards on the boulder-laid trail as we climb up through a series of zigzags before our path levels out at an area of red earth below small cliffs, giving us views back to the *degollada*.

From the red earth, our path runs along the lip of the *barranco* below the cliffs before turning left to climb up over rock and away from the ravine on a rough path to come alongside abandoned terraces. The tiled roof of a hut comes into view as our route follows the edge of terraces to pass behind the hut (Wp.9), from where we follow a rough donkey trail up between tumbled stone walls to come onto a dirt road.

It's a gentle stroll along the dirt road as it starts to run downhill to come past a steel barrier, and waypost, below the wall of an *embalse* (Wp.10 86M).

We now start to pay for all that downhill as we go up a rocked-off dirt road signed to 'El Refugio'. Coming up round the *embalse*, we face slopes of abandoned farm land stretching up to the horizon.

A rough path, well waymarked with white splodges, takes us up between the picturesque **Barranco del Ancón** and a large water channel. The steady, relentless ascent can distract from the beautiful views as we cross a metal water pipe and twin concrete canals several times before coming up to a tumbled cottage (Wp.11 108M). After the cottage the gradient eases for us to stroll up to a circular water tank (Wp.12) and cross the water channel to walk across to abandoned terraces. Now the ascent starts again as the white splodged path takes us up through the old terraces onto a steep section of the path which brings a white house into view.

Wp.13, El Refugio

A stiff climb between two concrete canals takes us past the white house and onto a dirt track, passing **Casa de los Abuelos** with the welcoming sight of **El Refugio** ahead; a final few metres bring us up to this unique hostelry (Wp.13 133M); unique if it is still a hostelry as ownership seems to change regularly.

From **El Refugio** we head up the dirt track to pass a goat farm on our left and a dirt track to the right (Wp.14).

For the adventurous we can short cut back to our start point by descending into **Barranco del Rey** on a donkey trail behind the goat farm, though unfortunately the continuation on the far slope has been long abandoned leading to a lively ascent - see map for paths which are linked by walking along the polished boulder watercourse.

Our choice is to continue up the dirt track to the **Ifonche** road (Wp.15 149M) to turn left and follow the tarmac. We drop down into the **Barranco del Rey**, the road swinging left across its watercourse (Wp.16 159M) where a **Vilaflor** walking route is signed off the road. A steep climb brings us up to **Bar/Rest El Dornajo** (Wp.17) for the possibility of refreshments before heading out on the narrow tarmac lane to our starting point (Wp.1 174M).

Tenerife's **GR131** long distance walking route is a welcome official addition to the island's extensive network of hiking routes. This final section from **Vilaflor** to **Arona** via **Ifonche** has a newly created trail which has opened up previously inaccessible areas to walkers; plus it's a route with a top class *típico* restaurant (**El Dornajo**) at approximately the half way point. While this route has a number of signs and wayposts, it still pays to read and follow the detailed walk description as a couple of important junctions are not signed, such as Wp.15.

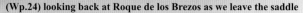

(Wp.24) looking back at Roque de los Brezos as we leave the saddle

For the first half of the route we're in pine forests, following a series of old trails that have been linked together to form part of the **GR131**, before descending to **Ifonche**. We then follow our Walk 16 'Fantasia' route, enjoying exceptional views until taking the newly-made **GR131** trail to link with our Walk 11 'Roque del Conde - Table Mountain' route for our finish in **Arona**. On the descent towards **Ifonche** there is a small vertigo risk on some sections of the 'Striding Edge' style descent, though the worst sections have sturdy wooden safety fences installed. Combining such a range of scenery, views, and refreshments this route is destined to become a modern classic of Tenerife.

Access by bus: Nº342 or 482 to **Vilaflor**. Nº480 or Nº482 for return from **Arona**.

Access by car: Ideally, arrange a two-car expedition, leaving one car in **Arona** and then driving the other car up to the parking area by the hotel and sports ground at Wp.4. At the end of the route you simply drive the first car up to pick up your second car. This is the most efficient arrangement, plus you cut out the first 1.3 kilometres of road walking with its 100+ metre ascent, quite the most boring and laborious section of the whole route.

If you are a 'one car' group, we suggest parking in **Arona** and catching the Nº482 or Nº474 bus for the ride up to **Vilaflor**.

The start of the walk for bus users
Arriving by bus, you'll be dropped off at the bottom of **Vilaflor** village by the petrol station (Wp.1 0M) from where we face a steady uphill slog along the

main road passing a number of bar/cafes before coming to the first street on our left (Wp.2). We could go up this street, but as it's extremely steep, our preferred route (walking or driving) is to continue up the main road to the second street (Wp.3) where we face a steep enough ascent before the gradient relents for us to continue up to the hotel where we find the first **GR131** signpost 'Ifonche 10.2km / Arona 16.7km' at the end of the parking area (Wp.4 30M), our start point for 'two car' groups.

GR131 sign at Wp.4

The sign nailed to the tree near Wp.5

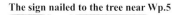

'Two Car' start for the main walking route

Leaving the parking area (0M) we go steadily uphill on the dirt track passing a track off to our right and vegetable plots before a steeper climb brings us up to a junction of tracks (Wp.5) where we go right following a 'Las Lajas' sign nailed to a tree.

It's a steep climb up the rough track bringing us to a roofed *embalse* before a steady ascent up to a **GR131** waypost (Wp.6 12M, 'Ifonche 9.2km').

Taking the new **GR131** trail, we head west through pine-covered slopes to a junction marked with a cairn (Wp.7 21M). We continue ahead on the main 'manicured' trail to cross a *barranco*.

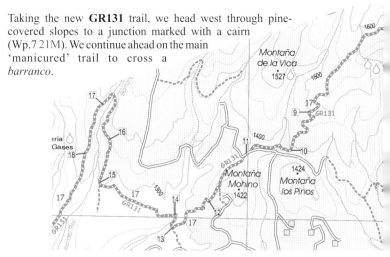

Then it's down into another ravine, followed by another climb onto the *lomo* (Wp.8) between ravines with a stone-built table and *mirador* views down over the southern vistas. Although our route is generally downhill all the way, it is punctuated by these *barranco* crossings, until we've crossed the largest, **Barranco del Rey**, directly above **Ifonche**. Passing another stone table amongst the pines, we continue down and up through another *barranco* before our descent stays on a *lomo*, bringing us down through a waymarked hairpin bend (Wp.9). Continuing down to a water change point below, we come onto a dirt track (Wp.10 65M) marked with a **GR131** waypost and a 'trail restrictions' sign. We are now amongst the dirt tracks above the **Ifonche** plateau often used by quad bikers, so watch out for traffic amongst these forested slopes! Going west, we pass a waypost 'Ifonche 6.7km' at a track junction shortly before coming to a clearing around a large pine, almost like a roundabout amongst the forest, where the dirt track heads down into a *barranco*.

We take the 'GR131' signed trail, leaving the dirt track behind (Wp.11 73M) to head steadily downhill through the trees. We pass a red and white waymark before our trail crosses a minor dirt track (Wp.12), coming from an abandoned cottage. Coming down the *lomo*, we arrive at its nose to overlook cultivated areas before heading down into the next ravine.

Two wayposts keep us on the trail where a water runoff could be confused for a walking route, before we descend to a junction (Wp.13) with a trail joining us from the left.

The Guajero stone bridge (Wp.14)

Now it's down into the *barranco* where a safety fence protects us from a vertiginous section before we drop down (literally) to the picturesque **Guajero** stone bridge (Wp.14).

The sheer-sided *barranco* along with the stone bridge presents some of the most dramatic scenery on this section of the **GR131**.

Climbing up out of the *barranco*, we cross an area of rock to head for a water channel with a cairn alongside a potato field above a modern house. Across the water channel, we continue up (WNW) across another rock sheet guided by red and white waymarks to come up to a water change point above a small reservoir. Previously we had been heading west and south-west downhill towards **Ifonche** but now we're heading west north-west in a steady climb away from **Ifonche** - it's tempting to be looking for a trail going left (south) but after dipping into and climbing out of a s m a l l *barranco* we come to a

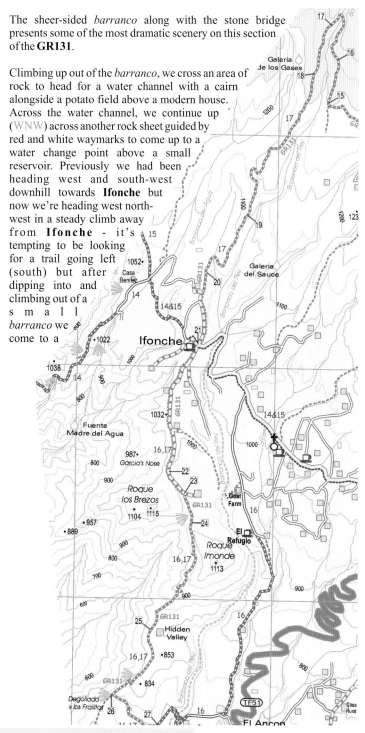

junction (Wp.15) where a trail does indeed head south - this is one junction that really should have a 'GR131' sign, as the correct trail is north, uphill.

Now our trail heads up the eastern side of **Barranco del Rey** in a steady climb where a red and white waymark (Wp.16) confirms we're on the correct route. We continue climbing until the trail dips down to cross the watercourse before climbing up the western side to the peak of the path (Wp.17 140M).

Now we have a comfortable downhill stroll as we head down the *lomo* between two ravines (S) to pass an *era* threshing circle (Wp.18 149M) as the ridge narrows to a 'striding edge' style descent, the ravine's walls dropping sheer beside the path. We need to pick our way carefully down the trail as fallen pine needles can make for slippery surfaces on the rock, and always stop if you want to look at this spectacular landscape. Wooden safety fences (Wp.19) protect us from a vertiginous section before dropping us down into a *barranco* and then climbing steeply up to a waypost (Wp.20) telling us the reassuring news that **Ifonche** is just 0.6kms ahead.

Reassuring news at Wp.20

We come onto a dirt track for an easy downhill stroll, the track becoming tarmacked before it finally drops us down to the crossroads outside **El Dornajo** (Wp.21 190M). To come across a well-recommended restaurant in the middle of wild countryside is an unusual event, so we take full advantage by stopping for lunch. Pork and rabbit are the specialties though there's not much for vegetarians.

From **El Dornajo** (following an enjoyable lunch so timings might be a tad slower than normal), we follow the route pioneered in our 'Fantasia' walk for over three kilometres, the official **GR131** having made this previously little-known trail into the equivalent of a walking motorway.

From the crossroads outside the restaurant (Wp.21 0M), we head south along a tarmac lane for an easy stroll, keeping to the main lane when branches go off to our left, the second at a cross - the start point for 'Fantasia' - to pass below a paraglider launch point (Wp.22 13M) at **García's Nose**. As **Roque de los Brezos** rises on our right, our lane starts to run downhill to its end at a farm with noisy dogs.

Here we are looking for a faint trail (Wp.23 15M) leaving the lane by a white-topped marker; the official path leaves the lane a hundred metres further down the lane but offers no better route out to the saddle between **Brezos** and **Imoque**. A myriad of faint paths, including the official one, lead across the broken ground to bring us over to the **GR131** signboard alongside the *era* on the saddle (Wp.24) giving us one of the most spectacular views in the south.

Our **GR131**/'Fantasia' trail resumes with a wooden safety fence as it heads down below the slopes of **Imoque** (S then SW) with a steep *barranco* developing on our right. The trail has been 'improved' by being slightly channelled to avoid a slip to the right, but the result is that with more walkers and water runoff, the channel has become littered with shale sized rocks making for a very picky descent; views are spectacular but always 'stop to look at the view'.

Underfoot conditions improve as we approach the *era* above the abandoned farm in 'hidden valley' (Wp.25 48M) for us to continue down on rock, stepped in places.

Our trail drops below the ridge line, cutting out the view, before emerging to *mirador* views and then dropping down to a junction on the **Degollada de los Frailitos** (Wp.26 64M).

Ahead is a new path to the northern descent from **Roque del Conde** while we follow the main trail left (SE) as it descends into a shallow valley beneath the lower slopes of **Roque del Conde**. After the earlier picky descent this is a relaxed downhill stroll following our 'Fantasia' route until we meet a 'GR131' waypost (Wp.27 76M) where 'Fantasia' continues ahead while we turn right on the new **GR131** trail which heads along the *lomo* (SE) between two *barrancos*.

We pass an *era* on our left just before the ruins of cottages alongside our solid rock trail after which our path descends to a new crossing of the **Barranco del Rey** (Wp.28).

Above the final *barranco* crossing (Wp.29)

Just above the ravine floor is a cairn seat, if you fancy a rest before climbing up onto another rock *lomo*. Our clear trail curves above the **Barranco del Rey**, protected by a wooden safety fence before it runs on to meet the **Roque del Conde** trail above the final ravine crossing (Wp.29).

Another descent to the *barranco* floor is followed by a steep ascent up the well-made trail to bring us onto the end of a small, steep street (Wp.30). From here we climb up to join the main street of **Vento**,

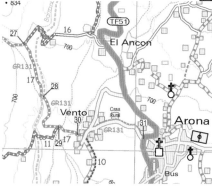

turn left and then right at the memorial for a final stroll along the quiet lane, passing a *casa rural* before coming down to the main road parking area above **Arona**'s town square (Wp.31) and the final 'GR131' signpost, as the long distance trail crossing the island ends its journey here with us.

Seen from **Vilaflor**, **Sombrero de Chasna**'s 'top-hat' peak is the highlight of the *caldera* rim with its 'sunlight throne' rising from pine-covered slopes. For its superb views over southern Tenerife, neighbouring islands and into the *caldera*, this is a 'must do' hike either on this itinerary or as part of 'Crater Rim Challenge'.

The final ascent onto the summit involves a short, easy, scramble (Wp.10) through a stone chimney that is a small inconvenience (not exposed, but support of hands needed) before experiencing the views. Our route follows reasonably distinct trails lavishly dotted with cairns. Be prepared for a lot of sun, intense at this altitude, even in the pine forest. Take enough water.

Access by car: Take the TF-21 road above **Vilaflor** to **Zona Recreativa Las Lajas** at Km58.5. There is ample parking in the recreation area though it can get busy with family picnics at weekends.

Access by bus: 'Tourist' Bus Nº342 from **Las Américas/Los Cristianos**, only one service per day. **Las Lajas** is an unmarked request bus stop so tell the driver when boarding. You could take Nº482 bus to **Vilaflor** and then a taxi to **Las Lajas**. If arriving by bus, see our Walks 19 descending to **Adeje** and 33&34 descending to **Vilaflor** for a walking finish to link with bus routes.

Starting in Las Lajas (Wp.1)

From the **Las Lajas** entrance (Wp.1 0M) on the TF-21, we stroll down the road (E) for 300 metres to where a track forks left off the road by a 'Las Lajas' sign (Wp.2 4M). Passing the vehicle barrier we climb gently (N) on the increasingly rough track with a *barranco* on our right, our track occasionally merging with the *barranco*'s watercourse. When our track swings sharply right by a pair of cairns a faint path joins from our left (Wp.3 12M).

Following the track right (SE), we turn left on a cairn-marked path (NNE) 250 metres later, where the *pista* is barred by a line of stones (Wp.4 15M).

A faint path joins our trail from the left as the gradient eases and we get our first views of the *caldera* rim ahead and **Sombrero** on our right. Crossing a watercourse, our pine-carpeted trail climbs out of the ravine bed (SSE) to traverse under a rock formation and the boundary line of the national park. Crossing another watercourse, we pass a bare-rock gully as our trail climbs toward another spur, where we come to a mapboard at a signposted T-junction (Wp.5 48M, see photo on next page). Our return route down to the road is to the right. We bear left for 'Cañada Blanca/Parador' on a stone-lined path

The junction at Wp.5

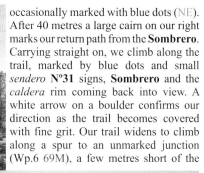

occasionally marked with blue dots (NE). After 40 metres a large cairn on our right marks our return path from the **Sombrero**. Carrying straight on, we climb along the trail, marked by blue dots and small *sendero* **Nº31** signs, **Sombrero** and the *caldera* rim coming back into view. A white arrow on a boulder confirms our direction as the trail becomes covered with fine grit. Our trail widens to climb along a spur to an unmarked junction (Wp.6 69M), a few metres short of the

Wp.7 at the circle of stones, Sombrero in view

caldera rim. Turning right (E), we now skirt the rim of the *caldera*, and the National Park (several signs), enjoying superb views of **Teide** and the crater, **Sombrero** and distant **Gran Canaria**. 230 metres later we come to a junction at a distinct circle of stones (Wp.7 74M) and a 'National Park' limits sign.

The trail ahead continues on to **Degollada de Ucanca** and **Parador** (see Walk 33), but we bear right to leave the *caldera* rim on a path heading directly towards **Sombrero** (SE). We follow the cairn-marked path as it runs through growths of *retama*, before another path joins from east (Wp.8 77M). Bearing right and then immediately left at a big cairn we maintain direction (SE) to come to a Y-junction with two large cairns (Wp.9 79M).

Now, to tackle **Sombrero**, we turn left and go toward a rock with white-and-blue paint, passing it to our left. We follow more paint-dot waymarks towards the summit (S). Passing a rocky outcrop on our right, we approach the main massif of **Sombrero**, spotting a clear paint-dot in the chimney of the north face - the chimney is our way up onto the top! As we climb up through the chimney (Wp.10 85M), an occasional support of hands comes into use before we emerge at the top. Once on the summit plateau, we maintain direction (S) to the southern-most point of **Sombrero** for the best views, but do memorize your way back to the chimney.

At Sombrero's southern rim (Wp.11)

The summit plateau is quite large and the terrain here rather confusing even with the paint-dot waymarks. Halfway across the plateau we pass a small stone windbreak before reaching the southern rim of **Sombrero de Chasna**, where there is a large cairn and a stone seat (Wp.11 92M) with panoramic views of **Gran Canaria**, the western islands, and Tenerife's southern coast.

For our return (0M) we retrace our steps to the Y-junction (Wp.9 14M), where we bear left (W), past the second of the two big cairns. Our path descends gently, snaking between bushes of *retama*, twice crossing a watercourse before encircling a distinct mushroom-shaped rock (Wp.12 18M). Soon after we cross (don't stay in the watercourse but cross it directly), then re-cross, the watercourse, at the edge of the sparse pine forest. 350 metres after the mushroom rock, we come to a Y-junction (large cairn), where we take the branch climbing to the right (Wp.13 28M). Two minutes later we join our outward path, 40 metres away from the T-junction at Wp.5.

Back at Wp.5, we carry straight on downhill (S), soon passing two stone windbreaks before our trail runs into a series of switchbacks. 70 metres after a two-metre tall cairn, at the edge of one switchback, we ignore a fainter path to the left, soon after which we catch our first glimpses of the main road. 70 metres after spotting the road we pass a right fork (a possible rough shortcut) to continue straight on to a T-junction, where Walk 33 joins from our left (Wp.14 55M). Turning right (N) we pass the shortcut path and cross a gully. Immediately after the gully we bear right at a Y-junction to pass two ruined huts before descending to a small pull-in and mapboard on the TF-21 beside a ruin (Wp.15 63M).

We have two choices to return to **Las Lajas**. Easiest is a boring slog up the main road (W) for 1.2kms back to the *zona recreativa*. A more interesting approach is the new connecting path to **Las Lajas**. From the mapboard, we descend to the watercourse to go through the tunnel under the road. At the end of the tunnel we climb up the stone steps onto a trail which then crosses a stream running from another tunnel. Here we bear right on an ascending dirt track, soon neatly lined with stones. 150 metres later, we turn left and descend down the steps onto a trail which sharply climbs on steps to almost touch the main road. Our trail crosses a pair of watercourses and then undulates through mellow ups and downs for us to reach the campsite at **Zona Recreativa Las Lajas** (85M).

19

The **Camino de Teresme** was once important for allowing trade of different products between coastal areas and higher-altitude regions. Our route follows this once significant route, which has recently been restored and waymarked, including interesting sections of a new trail. A savage ravine, the colourful volcanic cone of **Montaña Colorada** and the jaw-dropping panoramic view from **Boca del Paso** at the hike's finale are the highlights, though bear in mind the 1,800 metres descent is a challenge for one's knees! However, the route follows mostly very comfortable dirt tracks and paths until the viewpoint of **Boca del Paso**, from where a broad but rough trail plunges down to our destination in **Adeje**.

* in Adeje

Access by bus: Tourist bus Nº342 from **Playa de las Américas/Los Cristianos**. **Las Lajas** is a request stop so make sure you tell the driver when boarding; there is only one bus per day, but the timing is good.

Wp.1, 30 metres south of the mapboard

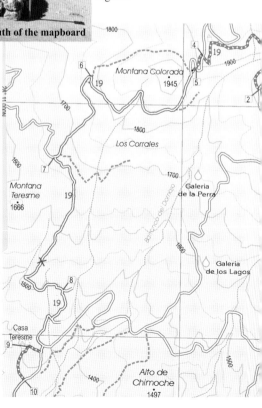

Alternatively, there's a more frequent service to **Vilaflor** (Nºs 474, 482), from where you could taxi to **Las Lajas**. Being a long linear route, it is not practical for hire car drivers.

Our starting point is **Zona Recreativa Las Lajas** (Km58.5 on the TF-21). Thirty metres south of the mapboard by the main stone hut (Wp.1 0M), we take the dirt track to the right (W) - signed 'PR TF 71 Camino de Teresme'.

Following the neat, gently descending track for nearly three kilometres, we cross a canal twice (26M & 32M), before turning sharp right onto a wayposted path (Wp.2 40M).

Turning right at Wp.2

We now traverse above a deep ravine (NE) to its right side on a clear path dotted by cairns. Crossing the watercourse, we walk up stream for a while, before crossing another watercourse (Wp.3 48M), after which our path swings west. This area has suffered in recent forest fires so it is interesting to see new branches of pines already sprouting!

We climb steadily away from the ravine (W) before the trail levels off and we continue in ups and downs to cross a cream-coloured bare-rock streambed. Our path widens to a trail before we cross a broad spur, after which it becomes a rough track descending to a breeze-block hut. The track circles the hut before coming to a dirt road (Wp.4 64M), which we cross to continue on a path. Re-crossing the dirt road (Wp.5 66M), our trail runs into a dirt track as we skirt the eastern flanks of **Montaña Colorada**.

Traversing of this volcanic formation is a highlight of our route, notably in the spring, when the slopes get covered by carpets of flowers in bloom. An overgrown dirt track then joins from our left hand side, while we keep circling the colourful volcano.

Skirting Montaña Colorada

Crossing a watercourse, our track swings south-west to continue along a *barranco* on our left. The coast of Tenerife and island of **La Gomera** come into our view for the first time as we pass an artisanal stump decorated with a waymark.

We pass a shortcut path to our left down the volcanic grit slope, before coming to a Y-junction, where we bear left (Wp.6 88M) to leave the track, which continues around the volcano. A few minutes later, we ignore a fainter track to the left, immediately after which we take the waymarked left branch at a T-junction of tracks (Wp.7 100M).

Casas de Teresme (Wp.9)

We enjoy views of **Montaña Teresme** before we pass a vehicle barrier, 300 metres after which the dirt track is crossed by a massive red pipe. We briefly emerge from the forest onto a meadow and then ignore a track climbing left to cross the red pipe (Wp.8 123M).

Five minutes later in a right U-bend, we again ignore a left-hand dirt track, before coming out onto the meadow again, spotting *casas* in the distance. Bearing right and again right 50 metres later, we take an access track to the ruined cottages of **Casas de Teresme** (Wp.9 135M) that are visible from the junction.

Our path swings (SW) around the abandoned farmstead and takes us back into the forest, where we recover the main track after 150 metres (Wp.10 140M). Bearing right, we descend gently along the track beside a silver pipe, before a faint track joins from our left (Wp.11). Crossing an old canal, then a couple of pipes, we ignore a track to the left, immediately after which we come to a sharp right U-bend (Wp.12 157M), where we turn left and continue on a track beside a thick pipe (SW). Two hundred metres later our track dwindles to a trail to come to a Y-junction, where we bear right, taking the waymarked branch. The path runs through a wood of young sparse pines, cistus dominating the slopes on both sides.

Our stone-lined path broadens before we reach a signposted Y-junction (Wp.13 171M), where we turn left for 'Adeje/El Aserradero'.

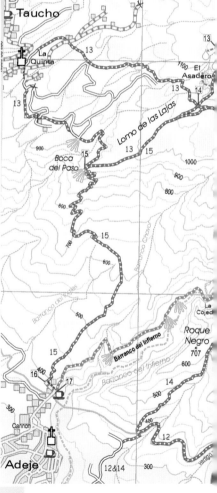

Ruins and a small reservoir come into view as our path traverses a steep slope above them. We pass an access track to the ruins and continue between walls, before crossing a shallow ravine bed choked with shrubs and cacti. Crossing a spur, we come to the 'La Quinta/Ifonche' crossroads (Wp.14 179M) set on a rock shelf, where we keep straight on.

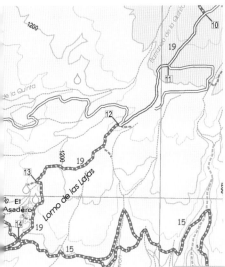

Our path (same as in Walk 15) runs alongside a carved canal, which we cross, descending along the **Lomo de las Lajas**. A path joins us from our left (Walk 13) as our trail changes from rock to dirt. Maintaining direction toward an antenna-topped peak, having views of terraces across a *barranco* on our right, a trail from **La Quinta** joins our path from the right just before we reach the stunning viewpoint of **Boca del Paso** (Wp.15 196M).

A signpost marks the beginning of our rough descent on a donkey trail. Great views of **Adeje** and the southern coast are a welcome distraction from the lengthy final descent. The trail is straight forward and there is nowhere to get lost as we make our way steadily down the vast slope toward two transmitter masts. Passing just next to the eastern mast, we zig-zag down onto a concrete lane (Wp.16 248M). Bearing left, we pass the **Barranco del Infierno** entrance hut, which is adjacent to **Bar/Rest Otelo** (Wp.17 250M) (open daily).

Wp.15 Boca del Paso, start of the rough descent

To find bus stops in **Adeje** follow **Calle de los Molinos** past **Bar Otelo** down for 300 metres to **Casa Fuerte** (fort). To reach the bus stop for the Nºs 447 & 448, carry straight on (**Calle Castillo**) for another 300 metres. For the Nºs 417, 460 and 473 buses, turn left at **Casa Fuerte** and continue past the church and *ayuntamiento* on **Calle Grande** to find bus stops at **Plaza Venezuela** (*Centro de Salud*).

20

Little-used paths take us down the western edge of the valley below **Santiago del Teide** through a mixture of bucolic countryside before coming onto a spectacular ridge for *mirador* views over the wild west of Tenerife, then descending on an old donkey trail to **Tamaimo**. Exceptional examples of endemic flora pack our route which soon leaves civilisation, though the distant sound of traffic is always with us.

This relatively leisurely linear walk can be made circular by using the final section of 'True Grit' up to **El Retamar**; then either 'True Grit' across the *malpaís* and its alternative finish to **Santiago del Teide**, or take the *camino rural* from **El Retamar** (our choice) up to **El Molledo** to join our outward route.

*For 'OK Corral' extension (optional) add 1 hour.   ** in Tamaimo

Access by bus: Service Nº460 links **Playa de las Américas** and **Icod de los Vinos** via **Santiago del Teide** and **Tamaimo**, a fascinating bus adventure in its own right. From **Puerto de la Cruz**, take the Nº325 or there's the Nº461 between **Los Gigantes** and **Tamaimo/Arguayo** and the Nº462 between **Los Gigantes** and **Guía de Isora**.

Access by car: There is usually on-street parking on the main street of **Santiago del Teide**, or carry on past the church to park alongside the shady picnic area on the left on the northern edge of the village.

Wp.2 at the ornate bridge

Our start point is the centre of **Santiago del Teide** by the **Masca** junction, opposite the church (Wp.1 0M). Strolling south along the pavement, we come to the ornate arch and bridge (Wp.2 5M) for the **Fuente de la Virgen**. The bridge takes us over a watercourse, then under a second arch we come onto the **Camino de la Virgen de Lourdes**. A dirt trail takes us across the meadow before we start to climb an out-flung spur of **Montaña Ijada**, where the route becomes a stone-laid donkey trail. The route is 'waymarked' by fourteen two metre high crosses, each with a plaque depicting a stage of the *Calvario*.

Past the first cross, there's an energetic climb as we follow the signed route after the third cross rather than taking the short cut to the sixth cross. At a spoil heap a dirt path goes straight ahead while we continue ascending on the stone-laid trail. The steady climb finally brings us to the fourteenth cross where the trail swings right to climb diagonally across the slope to a *mirador* at a hairpin bend overlooking the village. After taking in the views we ascend through the bend to make a last climbing traverse across the slope, which brings us up the flower-bedecked *ermita* (Wp.3 15M) set in a rose bower. Suitably breathless, we can admire the *ermita* and the views over **Santiago del Teide**, set off by the dramatic backdrop of the golden lichen-covered cliffs of **Montaña Ijada**.

Refreshed in soul if not in body, we pick our way back down the same route to **Santiago del Teide** (30M). Continuing south on the pavement we pass the garage to come to the signed *sendero* 'Puerto Santiago 6.7km' (Wp.4 32M), opposite **Bar Tropic II**, our last refreshment opportunity until **Tamaimo**.

Wp.4, stepping out on the broad trail

We step out along the broad grassy trail (S) with the slopes of **Montaña Ijada** away on our right, easy walking through this bucolic landscape of stone-walled fields only occasionally in cultivation. The main road has swung away east as we pass a copse of stately palms on our left and a collapsed terrace wall.

Here the gentle nature of our route changes as the trail narrows and drops down between high boulder walls on a lumpy stone-laid base, before continuing as a dirt path which runs alongside

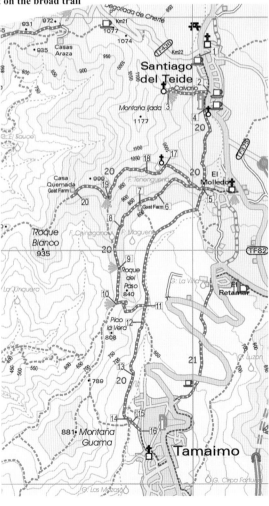

abandoned fields. Our trail is increasingly stone-littered as we descend gently towards **El Molledo**, looking over the village as our path runs across a large slab of rock at the end of a spur.

Wp.5; junction
with 'OK Corral' extension

The views then open up down to the ocean, the path becoming rough as it descends above cultivated plots to meet the wide stone-laid 'OK Corral' donkey trail.

Down below us is the second way marking sign for the continuation of the lower *sendero*, our alternative return route for a short circular walk, as we turn right to climb up (W) over rock to a path junction (Wp.5 44M) just past a 'Parque Rural Teno' sign, where 'OK Corral' takes the right fork while we go down to the left for 'Circular El Molledo'.

See the 'OK Corral' option at the end of the main walk description.

The rock and dirt trail with occasional stone-laid sections takes us steadily down the valley wall (W), great swathes of coloured rock and vertically grained rock 'fences' running down from the steep slopes above us. A steel water pipe runs alongside our route as we turn round a spur to see our trail running ahead around the valley wall. It is downhill on the rough path, crossing a boulder-choked gully (Wp.6 53M) before undulating along to the corrals and buildings (Wp.7 57M) of a goat farm.

The farm's large flocks of goats are cute, but they've churned up our path beyond the farm, so careful footwork is needed as we climb over a spur and into a pocket in the valley wall, before our route climbs higher above the valley floor to an outcrop of red rock making a natural *mirador* (Wp.8). From the outcrop we pass **Fuente Chiñagana** leaking water into two small pools, suitable only for animal consumption. Beyond the *fuente* we continue on the gritty, goat-churned path (S), dropping then climbing up to a saddle on the ridge (Wp.9 67M).

Once on the ridge before **Roque del Paso** we are treated to an impressive western panorama, including **Roque Blanco** and **Barranco de la Mancha de los Díaz** - camera essential.

From the saddle, our route drops steeply down the western side of **Roque del Paso** on a boulder-laid trail. Our trail becomes littered by rock flakes which have shattered from the rock face on our left before taking on an alternately flat then up-and-down nature to reach a junction on another saddle (Wp.10 77M), south of the peak. The views in this area are all five-star.

From the saddle we take a little-used path (E) which runs below the eroded southern face of **Morro de la Vera**. This path was made for the tunnel workers; there's a water canal that runs from **Tamaimo** to **Barranco de la Mancha de los Díaz**.

Goats keep much of the western section open, but our route has suffered from erosion and is becoming overgrown (secateurs may be useful). Concentration is necessary on the overgrown loose boulder trail, as we head downhill to a hairpin bend as we progress along traverses and through hairpin bends. After hairpin Nº9 we come below a large cave, the peak now hidden from view, and after hairpin Nº13 we encounter a large fallen rock, followed by a fallen terrace wall a little further on. Picking our way over the stones, we come back onto the path which winds down the slope to join the route of the lower *sendero* (Wp.11 89M).

For a short circular route - turn left (N) and follow the trail back up to El Molledo.

Turning right (S) we follow the narrow trail downhill alongside a steel water pipe; the pipe swinging left across the watercourse just before a faint walking trail (Wp.12) that follows the pipe. It's a steady trudge down the path to pass a large pine (Wp.13 100M) and a small garden before coming down to a junction (Wp.14 106M).

Here we turn left for 'Puerto Santiago', to skitter down a rock-laid slope into the *barranco*, then cross the watercourse onto slabs of rock to bear straight on at a path junction (Wp.15) which takes us up to the first houses of **Tamaimo** (Wp.16) and onto a tarmac street. At the end of the tiny street is a T-junction; left is steeply uphill and then right to climb up to the top of the town, but easier by far is to go right and then work our way through the old town to the main road (117M), refreshments and bus services.

Extension AN OK CORRAL (from Wp.5)
Casa Quemada goat farm offers a unique opportunity of seeing the landscapes beyond the northern wall of the valley. Here is an interesting diversion to extend your 'Wild West Tour' adventure.

From (Wp.5 0M) our route for **Casa Quemada** is the higher path to the right. We start the steady climb up around the edge of a bowl in the valley wall. Excellent views (stop to look) compensate for the energetic ascent on a mixture of stone-laid trail and rock slopes in reds and yellows. The gradient eases as we approach a corner in the bowl, just past which a Madonna statue and cross occupy a cave just above the path (Wp.17). Our trail leads us past the **Fuente Tenengueria** built in 1936, with a working water tap.

We resume our ascent of the plant-covered slope, our narrow path wriggling up towards the ridge line above. A stiff climb brings us up to two tiny walled terraces set in a small pocket in the valley wall (Wp.18), our route zigzagging steeply past them. In places the route is not clearly defined as it crosses sheets of rock, but a low stone wall keeps us on track to reach a purple rock *mirador*, just the place to take a break and enjoy the panoramic views across to **La Hoya**.

Scuttling beneath a precariously balanced large boulder, we descend into a pocket in the valley wall where our trail turns left above a large cleft. Grasses push in on the narrow path as we stroll (S) between the ridge and the long drop to the valley floor, the ridge gradually becoming less prominent as it comes down to meet our path (Wp.19 26M). Vistas open up across **Barranco Mancha de los Díaz**, and following the line of the ridge we zigzag down onto a saddle - the views are impressive!

From the saddle we go down the knobbly rock sheets, following a low boulder wall to reach a trail which we take down into the head of the *barranco*, a steep, almost staired descent which then levels out to follow a contour line around the bowl in the head of the *barranco*. We curve around towards abandoned terraces.

A climb up through the terraces takes us towards an overhanging rock outcrop, from where we enjoy stupendous views along the length of the west. A cairn of white-splashed rocks mark the path's continuation off the outcrop, leading us onto a clearly defined trail which heads towards the goat farm with its fences, gates and noisy guard dogs (chained). The couple who run this isolated agricultural enterprise 'commute' from **El Molledo**, carrying the goat feed with them!

A threshing circle (Wp.20 42M) alongside the corral makes an 'OK' *mirador*, but continuing down the spur towards **Roque Blanco** reveals dramatic views into **Barranco del Natero**, while if you look inland you'll see tourist hire cars lined up on the distant **Masca** road. We return by the same route.

Some walks have it all; varied landscapes, spectacular views, masses of endemic flora, great geology and refreshments. This is such a walk with the added advantage of *típicos* located just where you need them! Definitely a 'Western Classic'. While the new TF-1 road has impinged on our classic western tour, the classic donkey trail into **Arguayo** is reopened now that the works are completed. **Bar El Cercado** is closed meaning our **Arguayo** refreshments are now catered for by **Bar Tropic**. Down on the wide *barranco* floor we now have a pedestrian bridge to cross the new dual carriageway road, rather a contrast with the natural flora. Despite these changes, 'True Grit' remains a real 'Western Classic'.

Access by bus: Bus Nº460 from **Playa de las Américas**, and Nºs 461, 462 & 325 from **Los Gigantes** serve **Tamaimo** or for a less strenuous walk take the Nº462 bus as far as **Arguayo**, saving an hour of walking and the main 350 metre climb.

Access by car: Car drivers will find plenty of on-street parking around the T-junction in **Tamaimo**.

Our start (and finish) point is the T-junction in **Tamaimo** where the **Los Gigantes** TF-454 road meets the TF-82 main road coming round the mountains from **Guía de Isora**. We begin (Wp.1 0M) by walking south (S) on the TF-82 road, a gentle uphill stroll bringing us to **Calle La Rosa** on our left (Wp.2 3M). Turning left, we climb this steep street and pass **Calle La Ladera** on the left, to reach the last house Nº13, at the back of which the tarmac finishes.

We continue on a rough *picón* trail bounded by a rock boulder wall, the bulk of **Montaña del Ángel** looming over us on our right, and the peak of **La Hoya** with its antennae away on our left. Old rock walls line the path as we come up a ramp and step over a working water canal (Wp.3 7M), continuing to crunch upwards. Swinging

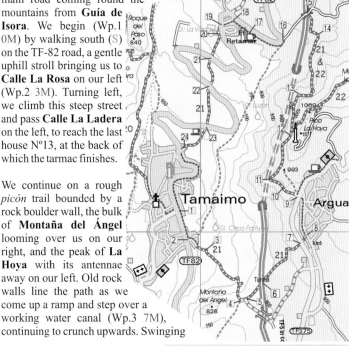

right round a Canarian pine brings us to an impressive *mirador*, a good place to get our breath back. Our steady ascent continues between pines, the boulder wall on our left splashed with a white paint boundary marker. The gradient begins to moderate and we look down into a valley populated by a showcase of endemic flora below **Montaña del Ángel** on our right as we head up into a bowl in the valley wall.

Now we face a loose scree, the boulder walls that accompanied us heading off left and right. Ignoring the faint path to the right, we follow the left wall (NE), a faint trail emerging as we progress. Coming to a hole in the wall, we swing right to continue climbing (S) which brings us onto a stone-laid donkey trail which takes us zigzagging upwards.

Above us, a cave in the slopes of **Montaña del Ángel** seems like a portal in a sci-fi movie - or it could be the effects of altitude and exertion! We continue our climb, terrace walls coming into view above us, and **Arguayo** stands out clearly on the ridge behind us. A final *tabaiba*-inhabited slope brings us up to join a fence of a garden and up to the end of a tarmac lane (Wp.4 32M) on top of the ridge alongside the terraces under **Montaña del Ángel**.

Descending from Wp.5 to the tunnel

We stroll along the lane for 60 metres before going left on a donkey trail (Wp.5), which descends between stone walls to a tunnel (Wp.6) under the new TF-1 road. Emerging on the east side of the tunnel, we climb to cross the TF-375 road (Wp.7), continuing straight on up along a garden wall to emerge in front of the closed

Bar El Cercado (Wp.8). We turn left to stroll along the street for 5 minutes until just after the museum **Centro Alfarero de Arguayo** we come onto the TF-375 by the bus stop and shelter. Diagonally left across the road is the continuation of 'True Grit' (Wp.9) going up a steep concrete lane with a staired centre. After all the climbing so far our choice is to take a short diversion by walking up the TF-375 to **Bar Tropic** (230 metres) for some rest & refreshments before tackling the next stage. After R&R, we stroll back down to the steep concrete lane to use the staired centre for the steep ascent (0M).

At Wp.9, our steep lane ahead

When the centre stair finishes, above a triangular *embalse* on our left, we go left onto a walking trail which passes between the terraces (W) and all the way to the bridge across the new motorway; this is also our 'Lasso La Hoya' route. Our route becomes a boulder-laid donkey trail, climbing up the steep slopes below the peak before the gradient moderates (Wp.10). We stroll under

The bridge (Wp.15) seen after Wp.12

sculpted cliffs and then swing north (Wp.11 12M) bringing views across the **Tamaimo** valley and to the knobbly peak of **Roque Blanco**. After an easy stroll the path changes to rock and we begin an energetic climb towards a group of eroded boulders (Wp.12

Boulder sentinels at Wp.13

19M), before descending gently towards a spur which runs down from the main ridge. The spur ends in a massive rock outcrop, suspended precipitously over the long drop to the valley floor. Large boulder sentinels guard each side of the path as it crosses the spur (Wp.13 24M).

Now the nature of our trail changes as the scar of the new TF-1 road dominates the valley below us. We go steeply down towards the valley floor, rich red rock dominating before we reach a section of old gold. Slopes and zig-zags take us down below the spur before the descent moderates beside old terraces (Wp.14) sitting above the new road with a stone walled trail to our right. We pass a group of pines to swing left (W) and ascend through an S-bend to the new bridge over the TF-1 (Wp.15).

From here our alternative finish continues north (see the end of text), 'Lasso La Hoya' goes east, while we cross the bridge to continue on a *picón* track (SW) to reach the TF-82 main road at a hairpin bend (Wp.16). Here we have a short stroll down the TF-82 to the service station's bright café with its *mirador* view for a second R&R opportunity (Wp.17).

After a second refreshment stop we walk down the main road to the village of **El Retamar** to turn left down a narrow street (Wp.18) which cuts off the main road's hairpin bend. On meeting the main road (Wp.19), we cross straight over to go down a tarmac lane, past **Casa de Tejas** (Wp.20) with its noisy dogs, beyond which the lane peters out and we go left onto a narrow walking trail. Although overgrown with grass, this boulder-laid donkey trail is in good condition, bringing us down past a horse and chickens enclosure to cross straight over the main road (Wp.21) to continue steeply down towards **Tamaimo**.

Endemic flora flourish as we swing left at a Canarian pine, giving views up to our earlier route below the peak of **La Hoya**, before crossing the main road again (Wp.22). Then we go left past a small rock outcrop to find concrete and metal water pipes which accompany our descent between stone walls with their gurgling. A gentle uphill, and the pipe disappears underground before reappearing as we stroll down to the main road (Wp.23) with **Restaurante**

Vista Guama a few metres to our right.

Again, we cross straight over the road to follow the donkey trail down past a roofed reservoir where the path is temporarily lost under rock rubble. In a few metres the trail reappears accompanied by two steel water pipes and we walk down to come onto a short street (Wp.24 81M) which brings us into the northern outskirts of **Tamaimo**.

A stroll down the main street provides plenty of opportunities for more refreshments before we reach our start point at the T-juncion with the **Los Gigantes** road. Although the walking time for this route is under three hours (165M), we expect your total time to be significantly longer if you've taken proper advantage of the refreshment stops!

Alternative Finish
Fifty metres east of the bridge and Wp.15 we take a track (N) paralleling the new TF-1 road. Approximately half way to the big new roundabout at the end of the TF-1 our track dips down left to pass through a tunnel under the new road. Once we are on the west of the road the TF-1 our track gradually moves away from the new road for us to strike the TF-375 near its TF-82 junction. From here we have a short stroll along the road to finish in **Santiago del Teide**.

Our original 'Lasso La Hoya' was a 'one hour up and down' circular, while our new route takes in the lava landscape below **La Hoya**, then climbs to **Las Manchas** where we take a stone-laid *calvario* trail beneath floriferous cliffs before climbing to the **Santo Ángel de la Garda** shrine for a mountain top stroll with magnificent views, before deciding between two alternative finish routes. While a 'pocket sized' short route, it encapsulates so much of adventuring in the west of Tenerife, we heartily recommend it.

Access by car: From the large roundabout at the end of the TF-1 take the TF-375 south passing **Las Manchas** to park near the football ground as we enter **Arguayo**, or on-street parking lower down the road near the village centre and **Bar Tropic**.

Access by bus: Nº462 **Guía de Isora - Los Gigantes** (weekdays only) runs through **Arguayo**. You can combine this route with Walk 21 'True Grit', to finish in **Tamaimo** with its more frequent bus services.

Bar Tropic (Wp.1)

La Hoya, meaning valley (!), is the sugar-loaf mountain dominating the eastern wall of the **Santiago-Tamaimo** valley. From our start at **Bar Tropic** (Wp.1 0M) we stroll down the pavement and then the road to meet the route of 'True Grit' (Wp.2 4M) opposite of the ethnographic museum where a steep, stair-

Approaching the bridge at Wp.8

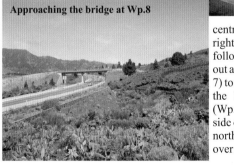

centred, concrete lane goes right (W) off the road. We now follow our 'True Grit' route out around **La Hoya** (Wps.3 to 7) to meet the dirt track next to the bridge across the TF-1 (Wp.8 42M). From the eastern side of the bridge a track heads north, while 'True Grit' heads over the asphalted bridge.

We take a broad track heading up the *picón* slopes of the lava field (E). It's a gruelling ascent on the loose *picón* track as it swings left and then right to head towards **Las Manchas**. Meeting the village's first houses (Wp.9 51M), we continue up onto the main street where we turn right to continue climbing steeply up past the church before turning right again (Wp.10 54M) in front of house Nº1 into a cul-de-sac marked by a large wooden cross on a red wall. We are now on the *calvario*, though it seems an inconspicuous route until we

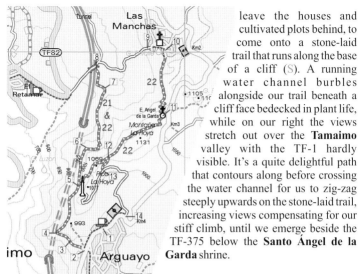

leave the houses and cultivated plots behind, to come onto a stone-laid trail that runs along the base of a cliff (S). A running water channel burbles alongside our trail beneath a cliff face bedecked in plant life, while on our right the views stretch out over the **Tamaimo** valley with the TF-1 hardly visible. It's a quite delightful path that contours along before crossing the water channel for us to zig-zag steeply upwards on the stone-laid trail, increasing views compensating for our stiff climb, until we emerge beside the TF-375 below the **Santo Ángel de la Garda** shrine.

Stepping up to the shrine (Wp.11 63M), we find that behind it is a dirt trail, at first indistinct, leading alongside the stone wall on its right side, toward a solitary pine and a pylon-topped crest (SW).

Leaving Wp.11, looking back at the shrine

We walk through the endemic flora heading around the north-western side of **Montaña La Hoya**; it's an easy trail - remember to stop to take in the spectacular views and plant life. This delightful stroll brings us along to a saddle on an orange shelf where the path swings onto the other side of the ridge and **Arguayo** comes into our view: here the trail splits (Wp.12 74M) giving us a choice of finishing routes.

For the easiest finish, we go left to drop down a steep narrow trail, its steepness and stone-littered surface making for a picky descent to the **La Hoya** access track (Wp.13 77M) where we go left to follow the track out past the football ground to the TF-375 (Wp.14 85M) where a downhill stroll brings us back to **Bar Tropic** (89M).

Alternatively, we go right off the ridge, where we also face a steep picky descent with the added challenge of crossing the water channel - I found sitting on the slab, swinging my legs round and jumping down to below the channel a safe if undignified method - before descending onto our outward route (Wp.5 80M) where going left we retrace our outward route back to the road and uphill to **Bar Tropic** (90M).

For this adventure we move away from the dramatic mountains of the west coast and into a gentler landscape of hills and valleys, though there's still plenty of uphill walking as we experience a surprising range of landscapes within two hours. Laurel forests used to cover vast areas of southern Europe and the Canary Islands, but few pockets of these once-mighty *laurisilva* woods remain. The middle section of this route passes through the eerie green stillness of one of these surviving pockets, and the entire route follows dirt roads, paths, *pistas forestales* and tarmac - not a rock climb in sight, resulting in a faster walking pace. With its unique flora, surreal landscapes and incredible views, this is a route you should not miss.

Bird lovers will spot endemic species about the pools (*charcas*) which have water after the winter rains. The pools were created by excavating the fertile soil which was then used to create fields and plantations in the coastal areas.

Access by bus: Reach **Bar/Rest Fleytas** on the Nº460 bus linking **Playa de las Américas** and **Icod de los Vinos**, the Nº360 from **Icod**, or the Nº325 from **Puerto de la Cruz/Los Gigantes**.

Looking over our route, shortly after the start

Access by car: Follow the TF-82 through **Santiago del Teide** to continue over the **Puerto de Erjos** pass to the TF-373 junction. Only use the **Bar/Rest Fleytas** car park if you are a customer and have asked permission to leave your car there; otherwise park between the restaurant and the TF-373 junction, where there is enough space.

Our start is at the cheerful **Bar/Rest Fleytas**. Leaving the bar (Wp.1 0M), we cross over the road to its southern side and go right to follow the road as it curves through a rock cutting. Just as we come to views down into a bucolic valley, we leave the tarmac on a dirt lane which drops down to our left (Wp.2).

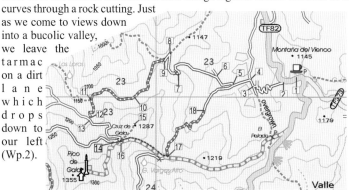

Springtime at the *charcas*

We stroll down the lane (W) between bushes of yellow broom with occasional glimpses into the disused quarrying area on our right. Passing a 'pencil' earth peak, we come down to a bend with views over the *charcas* and former quarrying area. The lane turns sharp left (S) for us to drop down through zigzags on an easy walking surface, possibly too water eroded for vehicles, until we come to a T-junction (Wp.3).

Through an idyllic landscape (Wps.3-4)

We take the dirt lane going right, coming to another junction in a few metres (Wp.4 10M) where we go left (W) for 'Punta de Teno'.

140 metres later the lane swings right and meets a waymarked track from our left (Wp.5), which is our return route. Immediately after this one we bear left to stay on the main lane which for the first hundred metres runs alongside a dirt wall with our return track on top of it. After passing a green lane off to our right (Wp.6), we start climbing quite steeply, overlooking fields that now occupy the former excavations. After stopping for a moment (15M) to look back at our route, we continue our ascent, the lane steadily climbing the valley side where white broom has now established itself amongst the yellow in this former quarrying area.

Our upward toil continues, the lane now cutting up through tree-heather covered slopes in a long, steep curve towards the south. Our *pista* now turns left (SE), the gradient moderating before a hairpin bend (Wp.7 23M) with an unused *pista* ahead as we pass a chain vehicle barrier to continue toiling upward, swinging right (N) below a slope of Canarian pines. On the final gradient the tree heather on our right gives way, allowing superb views across the valley and to **Mount Teide** which dominates the distant panorama. A final slog brings us onto the top of the ridge (Wp.8 30M), where a trail leads north off our *pista* along the ridge.

For a short diversion, climb the trail to a copse of pines and on as far as a rough rectangular marker post, from where there are fine views over **Erjos**; this trail continuing down towards the village, while we return to the *pista*.

On the ridge (Wp.8), we follow the *pista* south-west up a gentle gradient to large rocks, where the main lane finishes (Wp.9). A rough fire break trail runs up the ridge ahead, as we go right along a narrow path between rocks, immediately after which we enter an ancient, primeval laurel forest.

An easy, springy walking path winds along, climbing gently between mossy banks in this green, ancient forest environment. The trail comes up to follow a contour line, the steep slopes above and below us laurel-filled, the path unwinding beneath the high leaf canopy. We stroll through the eerie silence, twisting and turning with the folds in the steep valley wall, the atmosphere mystical. There are no views except for the trail ahead and the forest, and we must follow the path wherever it takes us.

We enter an area of older trees, some dead, marked by dark green, moss-covered boulders both alongside the path and clinging to the slopes above. Then ferns mark a lighter patch in the forest just before we come to a broken tree barring the path (Wp.10 38M - note that there is poor GPS coverage on the following section until Wp.11). We duck under and come through a rocky section before the path starts to climb, the forest becoming lighter as we climb from the depths to a crest in the path, then running downhill before swinging back (SW) as we negotiate another broken tree. Glimpses of tree-covered hillsides appear through the forest canopy as we ascend past fallen trees and a mossy outcrop, the path climbing steeply and tree heather replacing the laurels as we approach a junction in the path (Wp.11 44M).

We take the left hand path, climbing steeply over a crest before turning back into the forest again, seeming even darker now after that glimpse of sunshine. We follow the path into a small valley, the trail becoming boulder-laid as it climbs a narrow trench to a junction. The southern route is barred by a pattern of sticks, as we swing west to continue climbing the same narrow defile, the path zigzagging steeply up to a fallen stone marker post at the edge of the forest (Wp.12 50M). Dappled sunlight falls on us as we ascend through tree heathers, passing another stone marker to emerge into the sunshine and onto a *pista forestal* (Wp.13 52M).

We are on the 'wrong', western side of the ridge so we turn left to walk up the *pista* past a stately Canarian pine, and a yellow diamond walking sign pinned to a laurel. The steady uphill becomes steep as we swing up through an S-bend to another yellow diamond on a tree, then continue relentlessly up on this good walking surface until we climb through a bend to a gated and locked junction (Wp.14 60M). Above the junction are large signposts for 'El Pelado, El Saltadero and El Cercado' (the road that we've walked up). On a plinth by the junction is a brass plaque for **Cruz de Gala**, and a north pointer. For a short diversion a path leads up north-east to a heather-covered summit (Wp.15).

From the junction (Wp.14) we squeeze past, or climb up alongside, the locked gates to come down onto a tarmac lane (Wp.16) which serves the transmitter and forest look-out on the peak of **Mount Gala** to the south-west; a more challenging diversion rewarded with superb views.

Strolling down the tarmac lane, we take in the views over **Valle de Arriba** and **Mount Teide**, and notice the interesting *pista* which runs round the hillside in front of us, a finish on our 'Saddle Up & Round That Mountain' route.

If anything the panoramas improve as we come down the lane, a stark contrast to the atmosphere of the old forest. Far below us, the TF-82 winds up towards the **Puerto de Erjos** pass, and we come under an interesting rock outcrop and onto a saddle to get views of our starting point.

Wp.17 - we take the left-hand trail

At the end of the saddle we reach a signposted junction (Wp.17 68M; see *Alternative Finish* at the end of text), where the *pista forestal* (our Walk 24 'Saddle Up & Round That Mountain' route) runs to the right down the southern slope away from us.

Here we leave the tarmac and turn left taking the trail for 'San José de los Llanos/Erjos', which drops steadily down with early views of the *charcas*.

Descending briefly through an edge of a thin forest, the trail feeds into a track on a meadow (Wp.18 78M), which follows an elevated ridge between excavated slopes to meet our outward route at Wp.5, then it's back up the dirt lane to our start point and refreshments in **Bar/Rest Fleytas** (Wp.1 100M).

Alternative finish from Wp.17
Continue down the tarmac lane onto the TF-82 at **Puerto de Erjos** and then follow the main road north for 750 metres to **Bar/Rest Fleytas**, an easier downhill alternative finish with good views over the *charcas*, but take care to walk on the left side of the main road to face the oncoming traffic.

Breathtaking views combine with a floriferous environment to produce one of the most enjoyable routes in western Tenerife. An energetic start is rewarded by superb flora and exceptional views after climbing onto the saddle at **Degollada de la Mesa**. An optional ascent onto **Pico de la Mesa**, slightly vertiginous towards the top, brings us the most spectacular views in the region, and that's just the first third of our route. Easy walking takes us out to the **Cumbre de Bolico** and then through the forest to meet our Walk 23 'Laurel & Hardy' route at **Cruz de Gala**. From the junction at Wp.14 we return on the *pista forestal* and retrace our outward route back from Wp.5, but if you come by bus consider the Alternative finish (see the end of text) taking in **Charcas de Erjos** ponds, part of our 'Laurel & Hardy' route.

| 4 | 3H | 9 km | 450m / 450m | ↻ | 0 |

Our walking trail at Wp.1

Access by car: Park on the northern edge of **Santiago del Teide** alongside the recreation area, just before the road junction for **Valle de Arriba**.

Access by bus: Service Nº460 links **Playa de las Américas** and **Icod de los Vinos** via **Santiago del Teide**; from **Los Gigantes**, take the 462 or 325.

Our start is north of **Santiago del Teide**, just before the **Valle de Arriba** road junction (0M). We stroll alongside the main road with the antennae-topped **Pico de Gala** facing **Pico de la Mesa** across the saddle of **Degollada de la Mesa**, our first destination and yes, it is a long way up!

As the main road swings right we step off onto a walking trail (NW) currently signed 'no bicycles' (Wp.1 10M). Our narrow trail climbs steadily alongside the edge of the pine forest, then as the vegetation thins out we find a small *barranco* on our right. Endemic flora pushes in on our trail as we keep climbing before swinging right to cross the stream (Wp.2 16M). Now on the stream's northern side, we ascend through tree heather in a series of twists and turns to come onto a rock ledge (Wp.3). It's a relentless ascent, so take rests when you need them, thankfully relieved by expanding views and endemic flora.

An all too brief flat section is replaced by onwards and upwards, the vegetation thinning out as we ascend to another rock outcrop (Wp.4). Small cairns keep us on the trail as it climbs over sections of bare rock for us to come up onto the end of a *pista forestal* (Wp.5 36M - see photo on next page) by a signpost.

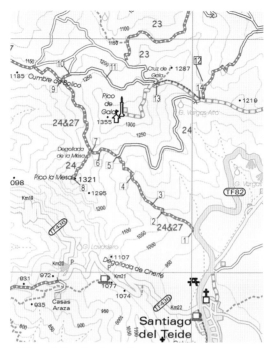

Wp.5, sign at the end of a *pista forestal*

From the end of the *pista* we take the walking trail heading (NW) up towards the saddle signed 'Punta de Teno', climbing past a rock outcrop (Wp.6) before the final ascent onto the **Degollada de la Mesa** (Wp.7 42M). Views west and south-east from each side of the saddle are impressive, but are as nothing compared to the views coming soon.

From the saddle (0M) our later route continues ahead, but first for a short diversion with splendid views we bear left on a dirt path that climbs (SW) through the shrubbery, waymarked with green paint. Gradually the path gets steeper and rockier until we turn across the head of a steep *barranco* where trees and plants are bedecked in orange lichen.

Our path becomes slightly vertiginous as we negotiate the final section of climb and scramble to achieve the **Pico de la Mesa** (Wp.8 15M). From this most orogenical and rather vertiginous summit, we have the most spectacular views in the west, if you can bear to look at them! Take care on the descent as both the rock and earth can be slippery and surprise the unwary.

Back on the saddle, there are a number of paths which can confuse walkers into thinking there is a route up **Pico de Gala**, and their attempts to find a trail makes these false paths more prominent. We look to follow (0M) the official yellow-and-white waymarked path (N), which becomes a green tunnel of tree heather before becoming a cobbled donkey trail.

Cobbled descents combine with smooth dirt sections to bring us out into the open with beautiful westward views of rugged mountains, deep *barrancos* and high meadows, the broad path now contouring around the head of a *barranco* to bring us to the **El Saltadero** junction of trails (Wp.9 10M), tucked between two low *sendero* posts.

The main signed trail continues ahead (NW) as we turn right (NE) onto a smaller path to climb up through the tree heathers onto a *pista forestal* where we go right to another junction (Wp.10). Again we turn right to walk up the broad *pista* as it steadily climbs between tree heather.

After the steady climb the gradient eases and **Mount Teide** is picturesquely framed between the tree heathers at one point, then later the red and white antennae on **Pico de Gala** are similarly framed (Wp.11) before we come into a region of poor GPS coverage. Finally we come to the peak of the dirt track for an easy stroll down to the **Cruz de Gala** junction (Wp.12 27M) where we meet our 'Laurel & Hardy' route. Squeezing past the steel gate, we come onto a tarmac lane (Wp.13) for an easy downhill stroll.

Below us, a *pista forestal* contours around the slopes and we meet its beginning at a **PR TF 51** signpost (Wp.14 35M). We go right to stroll down the *pista forestal* signed 'PR TF 51 Punta de Teno' to meet our outward trail at its end (Wp.5), then retrace our outward route down the beautiful valley to the main road (approx. 50 mins).

Views after Wp.14

Alternative finish
For hikers coming by bus we recommend bearing left at Wp.14 for an interesting linear route taking in the *charcas* and finishing at **Bar/Rest Fleytas** (see our Walk 23 'Laurel & Hardy' route from Wp.17).

A mixture of donkey trails and paths take us out onto the spectacular ridge which divides **Barranco Seco** from **Barranco de Masca**. 'Spectacular' is often overused, but not in this context as our safe but spectacular, and slightly vertiginous (but always broad enough), cobbled donkey trail takes us along the very spine of the ridge for the most impressive *mirador* viewpoints. One choice is to picnic at 'Hanging Rock' or further out at **Roque Cabezada** and return, though energetic hikers will be rewarded for the tough onward route onto the abandoned farmlands of **Finca Guergues**, a true rural idyll protected by fearsome cliffs. Remember that strolling around the old farmland slopes and descending to view the **Los Gigantes** cliffs requires a return ascent.

Time and distance is to the highest point of the ridge on top of the **Guergues** sloping plain - **Roque Cabezada**.

* No refreshments on the route, but **Autobar Cherfé** (on the **Degollada de Cherfé** pass) is almost always open, and a man selling fruit/drinks is sometimes parked in the *mirador* parking area.

Access by car: Turn off the TF-82 onto the TF-436 in **Santiago del Teide** signed to **Masca**. You must get out early if you're going to bag a parking place at the *mirador* just above **Casas de Araza** at Km20.3.

Access by bus: Technically, there's the Nº355 (**Santiago del Teide/Buenavista**) but it's not really convenient as the bus stop is 650 metres before Wp.1 (on a busy narrow road) and the minibus may be packed with **Masca** tourists, so it's probably best by car.

Our path to the right of the farm road (Wp.2)

From the *mirador* car park above **Casas de Araza** (Wp.1 0M) we walk down the tarmac until the main road swings sharp right and take a path on the right of the farm's concrete road next to a large opuntia and 'Finca Privada' sign (Wp.2). A path marked by stone cairns leads us (W) down through a maze of broom and willow-like Plocama pendula bushes.

The path occasionally divides, then rejoins just before we descend to a Y-junction (Wp.3 11M), where a stone-barred path from the farm feeds in from our left.

Bearing right, we follow the broad trail over the saddle and start to climb up over rock. Our trail takes us past **Barranco de los Sauces** on the left, which

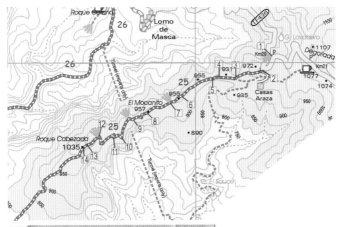

soon becomes a steep canyon. The rock-littered path rounds a spur to pass through a steel-and-pallet gate (Wp.4) signed 'Finca Privada', our onward route heading up a boulder-laid 'drawbridge' past a hole in a rock (Wp.5) and towards a distinct five-finger rock.

Bold goats (near Wp.6)

A climb over gold and then red rock (Wp.6) brings us onto a boulder-laid donkey trail which runs down onto a saddle, with a *mirador* view down over **Masca**, before climbing another 'drawbridge' to go steadily uphill again surrounded by breathtaking views. We climb towards the ridge ahead, views opening up past **Roque Blanco** down the west coast, the tabletop summit of **Montaña del Ángel** standing out in the distance on a clear day.

On the ridge

Our route swings north-west to a saddle between peaks, blood-red boulders lining the route up to a *mirador* (Wp.7 28M) on blood-red rock looking directly down on **Masca**, **Roque Catano** seemingly insignificant from this altitude. The route reverts to boulder-laid as it swings towards a craggy peak, our broad, sloping trail drawbridge-like as we climb to it. Once off the 'drawbridge' we lose the **Masca** views, as we steeply ascend the southern face of the peak, coming out onto more sheets of red rock, rock-fence remains dividing the sheets into rectangular sections.

A short downhill, then up again on a boulder-laid section to pass a cave before reaching the top of the ridge to climb up past an undercut small peak and onto a rock 'table' on the summit. This is our 'Picnic at Hanging Rock' site (Wp.8 35M), surrounded by stunning geology and breathtaking views. From here we have a good view ahead to the distinct peak of **Roque Cabezada**, the highest point of our route and the finish of our main itinerary.

The first section to 'Hanging Rock' was straight forward but now the route becomes more energetic, as after dropping down under a giant 'five-fingered hand' of rock to a steel gravity gate (Wp.9 44M), we face a steep zigzag climb back up onto the ridge for views down to **Masca**. Our path keeps climbing, steeply at first but then moderating before running along and swinging right to pass below a trio of caves (Wp.10 54M) before we start another steep zigzag ascent.

At the top of this ascent we come to a corner (Wp.11) featuring decorative small cairns, then a gentle section leads us to another steep climb that brings us onto the top of the ridge again and spectacular views (Wp.12 64M).

Our trail crosses to the west of the ridge running under a great hulk of rock, with sheer views on our right, before yet another steep zigzag climb brings us up to the summit of our route beside the peak (Wp.13).

Final switchbacks before Wp.13

After about 30 metres we bear off the main trail to the right and take one of the faint paths to climb, partly over bare rock onto the highest peak of the whole ridge, the unmarked **Roque Cabezada** (Wp.14 75M) offering spectacular views. A truly great place to relax.

After all that climbing on hard rock, the gently sloping green meadows and terraces rolling south-westwards are a welcome relief. A path leads down the plain to the remains of a hut, while lower down the sloping plateau you'll find the remains of houses, the now abandoned **Finca Guergues**.

Spectacular views abound from the edges of the plateau, but do remember that there's still plenty of climbing ahead on the return route and exploring down to the old farmsteads will add another 150 metres of ascents to your exertions for the return hike.

Barranco de Masca is one of Tenerife's most popular walks (and for a reason!), though this inevitably means there'll be hordes of others eager to tackle the most amazing ravine of the island.

We recommend making an early start ahead of the crowds (tour buses arrive around 10am). You're in for an unforgettable experience!

Negotiating one of the narrow ledges

You need to be fully fit to undertake the complete route to the beach and back. A good head for heights is essential as there are several exposed narrow ledges. After rains the path gets very slippery and authorities close the trail as the gorge fills with water quickly. If your fitness is in doubt, then you could walk down the *barranco* and catch the boat from the beach to **Los Gigantes**, Tel: 922 861918 or 922 862120 (different companies) for boat times and bookings before planning your walk. It's advisable to call the companies the day before to ask about weather conditions. If the sea is too rough the boat service may be cancelled.

At **Playa de Masca** there is a risk of landslides in the southern part of the beach (access at your own risk; note the signs).

*   we rate the 'downhill only' route finishing at the beach as '4 walker'

**   5.6km one-way, but feels longer, mainly due to the fact that several sections of the route are narrow or rather technical, making for slow progress. You may well need to wait for long lines of hikers coming towards you in order to pass a narrow stretch of path.

***   in **Masca**; and there may be vendors at the beach selling drinks from portable refrigerators

With its incredible landscape, **Masca** is one location where GPS is not suitable for navigation. The high ridges cut off satellites near the horizon and even with four or five vertical satellites, positional accuracy is poor. You can rely on the little metal signs that are placed along the gorge every 200 metres. These will reliably tell you where in the ravine you find yourself. For example, there are 28, 30, 32 etc. (32 = 3200 metres of distance from **Masca** village), the very last sign '56' is on a big boulder directly at the beach.

Our ideal scenario is to start from **Masca** by about 9 or 9:30am to get ahead of the crowds and take the boat back to **Los Gigantes** to avoid those frustrating moments on the return climb, often waiting till a long line of hikers in the opposite direction - often a group of about 20 people - clears the way. Furthermore, the boat back provides a unique perspective on the jaw-dropping sheer cliffs of **Teno**. A cold beverage on the deck combined with scenery of the mighty cliffs and there won't be anything more to wish for after a perfect day out hiking!

Access by bus: Technically you can catch the Nº355 from **Santiago del Teide**, the departure time making it possible to arrive on time on the Nº460 from **Playa de las Américas**. The last bus from **Masca** gives enough time to complete the route there and back, but for hikers coming by bus, the boat back to **Los Gigantes** is an attractive option. If you rely on buses and feel 'big', our Walk 27 'Scenic Ridge to Masca' is an appealing way of reaching **Masca**, complementing the close-range views in **Barranco de Masca** with fine panoramic vistas, making for the ultimate adventure, with the boat to **Los Gigantes** being the obvious choice.

Access by car: Take the TF-436 from **Santiago del Teide**, or **Buenavista** if arriving from the north, and park in the designated area above the village or on approved on-road parking. Start early as these spaces are rapidly filled.

Rather than give a step-by step commentary of the journey through this surreal landscape, we urge you to stay on the path. If you come to a seemingly impossible descent, then you have probably taken the wrong route when the path last divided, so backtrack and follow the alternative path. Use the small cairns of stones where they exist, and don't be surprised by steep climbs and descents as these do occur on the correct path, and expect some scrambling descents down giant rock falls.

Mapboard and steps at the start of our route

From the bus stop opposite **Bar Aquí Me Quedo** in

Masca (0M) we walk down into the village on the steep broad stone-paved walkway, passing **Rest La Fuente**, after which we take the steeper of the two walkways down past **Rest Chez Arlette**, spotting **Bar Blanky** in the distance. It's steeply down to rejoin the main paved route and walk out onto the southern promontory. 60 metres before **Bar Blanky** there's a mapboard at the steps down on the left (5M) which mark the start of the walking route.

You might like to recover from the twisty drive down to **Masca** in the bar while looking down on the first section of the route.

Stone steps lead us down from the mapboard and onto the 'path': a steep, slippery, boot-eroded route down into the *barranco*. Following the line of a rock 'fence', we skitter down to the palm trees where the path divides, where we take the left hand route to continue steeply down. The paths rejoin and the route becomes a little easier as it winds along the northern side of the *barranco*, a section of stone stairs assisting our descent to abandoned terraces. The massive, sheer-sided bulk of **Roque Catano** looms over us as we come down a stone defile. Our path winds down past large rocks onto an outcrop overlooking a wooden bridge, then a tricky, vertiginous descent brings us down onto the bridge (25M). Across the bridge, a steep climb followed by a narrow path (W) brings us opposite **Roque Catano**, the *barranco* dropping far below us on the right. Walled terraces, some cultivated for grapes, line the southern wall of the canyon as we reach a section where the path narrows dramatically for a vertiginous traverse across a rock slope followed by a scramble, the path then widening to a narrow walking trail as we descend past abandoned terraces and a stone seat under a palm tree. If you're concerned about the nature of the route this far, take a break in this picturesque spot before heading back to **Masca**.

The path narrows after the terraces and drops down steeply to the *barranco* floor which we cross through a dense bamboo thicket. Up past a large rock, we come onto a proper path which makes for relaxed walking as the ravine opens up around us, walled terraces forming a stair on the *barranco* wall as we come to a stone seat, set beneath a shady palm. We now begin a serious descent down rock and boulder slopes to pass under a large rock.

The canyon narrows, sheer walls almost closing over us as we descend to the watercourse by a large 'cubist' boulder.

Spectacular rock arch, about 1.5km from beach

We continue downhill on the northern side of the watercourse to curve under a huge boulder, a steep descent on boulders polished by hikers' boots. After this narrow defile, the *barranco* opens out as we come below veined cliffs on polished rock sheets towards a low dam wall. Across the watercourse, we continue down to the 'plain' where another ravine joins us from the north (59M).

Before stepping over the canal at the left of the dam wall and taking the steps down to the *barranco* floor, take a moment to appreciate the beauty of this area, as ahead of us lies the 'labyrinth'. Our path, marked by the brown scuffing of boots, meanders down the floor of the *barranco* as it narrows. Massive chunks of rock dam the defile in this section, and we go under the first of these rock falls, beneath an upended cone of rock (watch out for the large hole alongside the path, big enough to swallow the largest hiker).

We scramble down and then across the *barranco* floor to another rock fall. Steeply down the escarpment beside a photogenic waterfall and pool, we then meander across the stream to climb up, following the tortuous route of the defile. Sheer rock walls fly up hundreds of metres above us as we follow the path, marked by a small cairn of stones, to the unlikely sight of a fence. The ravine turns through ninety degrees, and we curve round a large rock to the even more unlikely sight of a green and yellow metal gate, propped open across our path. Again we drop down to the grey pebble floor as the path takes us over the watercourse.

Ahead, sunlight streams into the *barranco* where it widens. It's steeply down across another rock fall blocking the ravine, crossing the floor again to yet another giant rock fall. This descent is more like caving as we emerge below the fall, to walk down past a stone stair which leads up to the water canal built in the southern wall. Down two more rock falls, we eventually reach a sunlit rock promontory (100M).

Though it seems as if we must be nearing the sea, this is a false dawn. As the ravine widens, another joins ours from the north, creating an airy sunlit area in contrast to the narrow defile we've just come through. We realise that there's still a lot of *barranco* to go before we reach the sea. As you begin to appreciate the nature of this *barranco*, you won't be surprised to find the defile twisting this way and that below immense sheer walls, giant rock falls often with scrambling descents being the norm rather than the exception.

Often, the path divides and every now and then we seem to pick the most difficult route. Just as you think that this seemingly endless ravine will go on for ever we come to the hopeful sign of abandoned terraces on the southern wall (155M).

After zigzagging down the terraces and scrambling onto the floor, we climb up the rocks to a turn in the *barranco*. There's blue sky ahead! In our excitement we take the wrong trail along the *barranco* floor, including a 'slide and jump' descent through a massive rock fall. We stagger across the large pebble rocks to reach the beach (174M).

Looking inland; nearing the beach

Families of friendly cats share our lunch as we relax on this bay enclosed by sheer cliffs with its single holiday home.

... awaiting a sea-borne release ...

Several tourist excursion boats call in, their occupants lurching about on deck or jumping into the sea.

If you pre-booked a boat ride to **Los Gigantes**, take the walkway out to 'pimple island' and join the crowd awaiting a sea-borne release.

Our return (0M) to **Masca** is tougher than the descent as we face a strenuous 600-metre climb in altitude. After R&R, we set off on the return journey, following a steel water pipe up the south side of the *barranco*, to bring us onto abandoned terraces which bypass our 'slide and jump' descent of our downward route. However, our descent from the terraces is a scramble down a rock wall just past the rock fall, followed by a slippery traverse across rock sheets and back onto our downward route. This path is easily missed when coming down the *barranco*.

Well into the labyrinth, we take a break (35M), having already climbed high up the northern wall. We take another break (61M), the *barranco* echoing in various languages, 'How much further is it?' from those on the downward route. We reach the stone stair up to the water canal (89M) and then avoid the 'slide and drop into a pool'(105M) by taking the path up the south side of a huge rock fall. Past the dam, and we sink thankfully onto the stone seat under the palm (120M), the abandoned terraces reminding us that we are not too far from the village.

We reach another stone seat under a palm (131M) at the top of the lawned terraces, and soon after (141M) the village of **Masca** comes into sight, high up and far away, as we take care on the vertiginous sections of the path, reaching the wooden bridge (146M). The section after the bridge is the steepest part of our return. We labour upwards, inspired by survival instinct and the sight of **Bar Blanky** high above us. These grit slopes are as potentially treacherous uphill as down, but we reach the paved section of the stairs to emerge by the mapboard onto the paved walkway having taken almost exactly the same time as on our downward route (170M).

In one minute more, we totter into **Bar Blanky**, the *agua con gas* tasting unbelievable good, where we ponder our new skills as stegophilists.

Spectacular ridge-top *mirador* views reward our 350 metre ascent at the start of this Western Classic route, followed by an easy descent to the **Mirador Café** at **Cruz de Hilda** overlooking **Masca** village with a final trail descent to **La Vica** from where it's a road stroll to the famous village.

3 · 2½ H · 8 km · 420m / 710m · one way · 3

Access by bus: Service N°460 links **Playa de las Américas** and **Icod de los Vinos** via **Santiago del Teide**; from **Los Gigantes**, take N°462 or 325. Line 355 from **Masca** runs between **Santiago del Teide/Buenavista del Norte**.

Access by car: Park on the northern edge of **Santiago del Teide** alongside the recreation area, just before the road junction for **Valle de Arriba**. Return from **Masca** via bus N°355.

We start out from the café picnic area just north of the church (Wp.1 0M) to stroll along the **Icod** road (TF-82), passing the **Valle de Arriba** junction and keeping to the left side where a path, later broadening to a track, lines the main road. When the road swings right, we step off onto a trail signed 'no bicycles' (Wp.2 10M). Our trail skirts the edge of a pine forest on our right and heads up the side of a steadily steepening *barranco*, crossing the watercourse (Wp.3 16M) to the northern side where the trail steepens. It's a steady slog onwards and upwards across the rock sections before we emerge onto the end of a *pista forestal* (Wp.4 36M) where we join the **PR TF 51** trail.

On the Degollada de la Mesa (Wp.5)

Our rocky onward trail is signed 'Punta de Teno' off the end of the *pista* for a steep climb up to the reddish top of the ridge where we step out onto the **Degollada de la Mesa** (Wp.5 42M) - see our 'Saddle Up and Round That

Contouring around the massive bowl (Wp.6)

Mountain' route if you want to climb **Pico de la Mesa** on our left.

Views from the *degollada* are spectacular, more spectacular still if you ascend **Pico de la Mesa**, as we follow the trail down off the saddle (N) to start contouring (0M) around the massive bowl at the head of a *barranco*. Our broad trail contours around to bring us to the **El Saltadero** junction (Wp.6 10M) where our 'Saddle Up and Round That Mountain' route goes right up the narrower trail marked 'wrong way' between the two stumpy posts.

We continue straight ahead on the main trail, an easy earth path amongst tree heathers bringing us along to the strange sight of 'mesh nets' strung to collect condensation (Wp.7 14M); here we ignore a minor path on the left and continue along the main path through an enchanting forest with lichen-covered trees.

We drop down the trail to a small meadow with a signed junction on a broad *pista forestal* (Wp.8 16M) with a short concreted section.

Maintaining direction, we stroll across the meadow past a ruin where we ignore a minor path off left and dip back into the forest.

We're into tree heather as we make our way along the ridge before coming to a path junction (Wp.9 22M) where we keep right, to drop down the northern slope in a steep descent before the gradient eases.

A wonderful viewpoint on the ridge

We emerge from the tree heather onto the top of the ridge before a short climb, the first distinct one after **Degollada de la Mesa**, brings us to a *mirador* viewpoint on a bare ochre-coloured rock (Wp.10 38M) overlooking the **Masca** village and *barranco*.

Continuing along the ridge trail we are again in green 'tree heather' tunnels (poor GPS reception & slippery when wet) as we descend along the northern face before emerging onto another western viewpoint where we can almost see the café at **Cruz de Hilda**, the **Masca** road now invitingly near below us. Another descent on the northern face of the ridge is followed by a second brief climb to cross a small saddle onto the western face (Wp.11 52M) with yet again great views. After a sharp right bend we are heading away from the café to traverse a slope strewn by agave and prickly pear and skitter down onto a saddle with a four-way trail junction (Wp.12 58M) where we leave the **PR TF 51** heading to 'Punta de Teno'. To the left is our onward trail as we join the **PR TF 59** for 'Masca'.

Our trail swings left (SSE) for an easy descent below our earlier route as we contour along beneath the ridge on a broad donkey trail supported by rock walls, the valley below us coming slowly up to join us as we finally go down a paved slope to join the **Masca** road behind the *mirador* café (Wp.13 78M) on the **Cruz de Hilda**; note the small lane (*camino rural*) just north of the café - our onward route.

It would be a shame to ignore this ideally situated refreshment stop. In good weather, enjoy refreshments while drinking in the views down to **Masca** village before setting off on our final stage. From the **Mirador Café** (0M) we take the *camino rural* serving a pair of houses and shortly before reaching them, we drop off the tarmac onto a walking trail (Wp.14 2M) to start a picky descent down through small, mostly abandoned, terraces. A spring running across the trail makes for a soggy section after which it's all steadily downhill on the narrow path until it runs out onto a paved track (Wp.15) that drops us down into the hamlet of **La Vica**, joining the **Masca** road by the **Bar/Rest Masca** (Wp.16 13M). Turning left, we have a downhill stroll on the tarmac, looking out for the traffic, before the final uphill to the entrance to **Masca** village and the bus stop (Wp.17 25M).

Bus N°355 serves **Masca** until late afternoon, so depending on how quickly you've completed the route, you may well find time to explore the start of the **Barranco de Masca**, look round the tourist shops, or to relax in the bars and restaurants, or perhaps the welcoming shady plaza. Of all the bars around here, **Bar Blanky** offers the best views, thanks to its location on a rock promontory.

Las Cañadas is a big crater with the emphasis on BIG. Just drive from **Boca Tauce** to **El Portillo** to see how big this region is. It's just as big on foot, but being in direct touch with this amazing landscape means that the visual illusions are greater. In **Las Cañadas** everywhere looks closer than it is; in fact much closer, as your eyes foreshorten the large distances. Look at **Mount Teide** - it seems as if you could just reach out and touch it! 'Toffee Mountain', or **Montaña Majúa**, is our introduction to walking in these high altitudes (2000+ metres) in the western sector of the National Park and if our description tends towards describing the scenery in confectionery terms then blame it on the thin air.

In the second part of our route, we visit **El Sanatorio**, the isolated and now neglected if mysteriously-looking cluster of buildings, once constructed with high hopes for treating various ailments. Whether arriving by bus or car, we recommend that you take a ten to twenty minute break when arriving at this altitude to let your body acclimatise before starting walking.

Mouflon restrictions: Due to mouflon control, this route is <u>closed</u> when the restrictions are in place. See page 10 for details.

Note that in spring and early summer bee hives are sited alongside the route, so the route is not recommended if you are allergic to bee stings.

3 | 3H | 12 km | 300m * 300m | ↻ | 1**

* 200m of ascent and descent if opting to bypass **Majúa** summit, bearing left from Wp.9
** at the **Parador Café**

Access by car: Take the TF-21 to **Las Cañadas** to park at the **Parador Hotel/Café** or opposite the road at **Mirador de la Ruleta**.

Our *sendero*, Wp.1

Access by bus: N°342 from **Playa de las Américas** and **Los Cristianos** or N°348 from **Puerto de la Cruz** will take you to the **Parador**, from where you wander over to our start point at the café terrace. There's only one departure and return of these routes each day, so make sure you don't miss your bus!

From the café, we walk past the hotel entrance and set off down the access road. Keeping an eye to our right, we spot a gap in crash barriers and signposts at the start of *sendero* **N°19** (Wp.1 3M) walking trail. We're heading east towards a light toffee-coloured lava flow, on a distinct trail neatly lined by stones.

We pass a stone windbreak, then another one nested in a depression (Wp.2 7M) before coming up to the 'light toffee' lava wall where our trail swings north.

We follow the well-maintained trail as it skirts the lava wall (N). Leaving the first lava wall behind we cross a plain (Wp.3 14M) in a ruler-like straight line towards another lava flow. Coming below the lava (Wp.4 21M), more toffee than caramac this time, we skirt this new lava flow. It's an easy stroll to come between two large rocks (Wp.5 26M) before coming to an interestingly veined rock on the right of our path (Wp.6 31M), seemingly a laminate of various rocks.

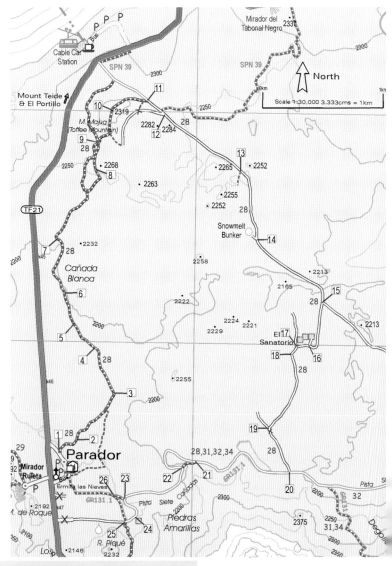

Our sandy path, rather like dune walking, moves out from the lava wall for a while before curving back towards an obsidian finger of rock (Wp.7 40M) followed by a small windbreak. Our path starts to ascend as the 'crunchy bar' coloured mound of **Montaña Majúa** comes into view, with a small valley on our right.

Wp.8 - Approaching Majúa

We come into a broken landscape of spiky rock outcrops before sticking to the obvious branch at a crossroads with an old, very faint path.

Our path climbs to pass between two hillocks (Wp.8 53M) where it levels off for us to spot the two paths climbing **Majúa** from this side.

Entering and leaving a short section signed 'Danger - Beehives' (in the honey season), we come to a junction (Wp.9 46M) where the main *sendero* swings left, while we bear right following a minor path heading steadily up towards the rounded peak where we reach the trig point (Wp.10 55M and 2353m).

Optionally, to avoid the climb to the peak, bear left at Wp.9 and follow the official trail to a **Sanatorio/Parador** junction where you join a dirt track, which runs in south-easterly direction to join our route at Wp.11.

From the trig point of 'Toffee Mountain' (0M) we go gently uphill (NE), maintaining direction, to cross the peak, then take the faint walking trail to the right (E), which becomes more obvious and drops down towards the **Pista Sanatorio**. Before descending, the roofs of the **Sanatorio**, our next destination, are visible away to the south-east.

We come down the trail to join the **Sanatorio** dirt track (Wp.11 7M), then we pass three metal covers along with *sendero* **Nº39** on our left, just before a junction where another *pista* goes off to our right (Wp.12 10M). **Pista Sanatorio** (trail **Nº16**) has a good walking surface, allowing us to make relaxed progress while taking in the subtle colourations of the rock formations in this region as we bowl along the *pista* to pass a track (signed 'Beekeepers only' in the honey season) off to our right (Wp.13 23M) just before our route curves right to run gently downhill.

We come down to a strange sight at a junction (Wp.14 33M) from where a bunker appears to have been concealed in a rock mound. If you take a couple of minutes to walk up to the locked door you'll see that the 'bunker' contains the large pipes of the system used to capture the snow-melt off **Mount Teide**; those metal covers are also part of this water system. Leaving the 'bunker' behind, we stroll down a straight section of the track before passing another 'Beekeepers only' track off to our left (Wp.15 46M).

Wp.16, at the Sanatorio

The **Sanatorio** roofs come into view on our right just before our *pista* curves between large rocks to the **Sanatorio** entrance (Wp.16 54M), just the place for a pleasant break after that power walking.

The **Sanatorio** was planned with the idea of catering for patients with respiratory diseases coming from colder countries, to take advantage of the dry air and favourable climate, then thought to have miraculous effects. However, it was actually never finished due to later advances in medical research that offered more efficient ways of treatment.

From the **Sanatorio** (0M), we continue on the *pista*, passing another entrance to the compound, then 100 metres later a path and a track off to our right (Wp.17), followed by another track off to our right (Wp.18) as our *pista* swings left (S), the **Las Cañadas** cliff wall rising ahead of us. An easy stroll brings us past a track on our right (Wp.19 15M) to negotiate a metal barrier across the main *pista* - hurdle over if tall enough, or duck under - before we come down to the **Siete Cañadas** *pista* (Wp.20 22M), beneath the crater rim.

If you're looking at your GPS in this location, you might notice it producing strange readings. The vertical escarpment cuts off satellite reception to the south, giving unreliable readings; not that you need any navigation devices for the next stage, along the **Siete Cañadas** *pista* heading west.

We turn right to join this walking motorway of **Las Cañadas** for an easy stroll as it climbs and twists along below **Montaña Guajara**, coming to a shortcut walking trail that cuts out a long loop of the *pista* (Wp.21 39M; near a metal cover) before rejoining the *pista* (Wp.22). We come to a left curve with panoramic views down over the **Parador** (Wp.23 53M, 40 metres after a wooden post), where another shortcut trail descends steeply down onto the plain. Staying on the *pista*, it's gently downhill as we curve left and then right, passing a vehicle barrier just before the black stone hut (Wp.24 57M).

100 metres after the hut we take the signed trail off to the right (Wp.25 59M) that leads to the **Parador**, the shortcut trail joining us (Wp.26 62M) where the main trail leaves the lava wall. Following the trail across the plain for a few more minutes brings us back to our starting point on the café terrace, three hours (180M) from beginning our adventure.

Walking routes don't have to be excessively long or strenuous to be spectacular. **Roques de García** is an accessible classic, within most people's easy compass. Spectacular geology gives an interesting viewpoint on the **Las Cañadas** region in a compact tour. The whole itinerary follows National Park official *sendero* **Nº3**, so the metal waymarks with number '3' along the way can be used to confirm the route. Walk the route in the direction we take, as the reverse direction involves a descent from the **Mirador de la Ruleta**, where boot erosion makes for a slippery, potentially hazardous, steep descent; much easier to climb than descend. Don't be concerned if, on arrival, you're confronted by hordes of picture-eager tourists. Most of them remain within a one-hundred-metre radius from the roundabout. Tip: late afternoon, when the tour buses and tourists are gone, there's absolute tranquillity accompanied by the low late-afternoon sun, to snatch perfect photos while experiencing this unique land of bizarre rocks and crags alone.

Mouflon restrictions: due to mouflon control, this route is <u>closed</u> when the restrictions are in place. See page 10 for details.

'God's Finger' (see Wp.2)

3 | 1¼ H | 4 km | 170m / 170m | ↻ | 1*

* at the Parador Café

Access by bus: N°342 from **Playa de las Américas** & **Los Cristianos**, N°348 from **Puerto de la Cruz**; there's only one departure and return of these services each day, so make sure you don't miss your bus!

Access by car: Parking in the National Park is quite restricted so it's best to arrive early (before 11.00am), or later (after 16.00) at the large **Mirador de la Ruleta** car park, or you can park opposite the main road at the **Parador**.

From the *mirador* roundabout, viewing paths lead up to the left and right - not part of our route - to give spectacular views down over the **Llano de Ucanca** plain and lava fields. We start from the north of the roundabout (Wp.1 0M), following the well-trodden path (N) alongside the chain on our left for a pleasant stroll to come below the impressive and much photographed symbol of the National Park, the **Roque Cinchado** a.k.a. **God's Finger** (Wp.2) on our left. Along the chain, our path curves left (Wp.3 - with an option to go left to a viewpoint over the **Ucanca** plain), becoming very rocky as we come under cliff walls. The rocky surface gives way to grey sand as we head north-west to pass between a lava field on our right and the impressive rock formations on our left.

A short climb (Wp.4) brings us up under the rocks and alongside an area of dark grey 'hippo-backed' lava field on our right. We curve left around rock pinnacles to face a large wind-sculpted rock formation just before passing a mapboard at a junction with *sendero* **Nº23** (Wp.5 17M), a 'boot-destroying' rough lava trail leading to **Pico Viejo**. Bearing left, we come to a natural viewpoint 100 metres later, where we climb to the right of the rock formation to a small natural *mirador* (Wp.6), where our path levels out. We start our descent down towards the plain, our path swinging left (S), the loose rock-and-scree surface making for a slow, picky descent, though alleviated by log steps on the steepest sections. A remarkable 'tree root' system of knotted lava is becoming visible on our right where it has solidified in the midst of tumbling down between the rock pinnacles.

Finally, the scree-covered path descent ends at the start of another hippo-backed lava field (Wp.7), making for easier progress. 120 metres later our trail swings left as we overlook the **Ucanca** plain (Wp.8) and pass examples of Teide wallflower (Erysimum scoparium) before moving across to the east of the lava field to pass below a jagged rock formation (Wp.9). We come under buttress-like rock projections, the self-shattering pillars soaring surreally skywards, before leaving the hippo-backed lava on our right, to come down onto a plain (Wp.10 45M).

Now it's an easy stroll along the grey sand path which brings us to a junction with trail **Nº26** across **Llano de Ucanca** off to the right (Wp.11 50M). We turn left towards the 'Cathedral', a Gaudiesque volcanic creation rising over one hundred metres out of the plain. Keeping left, we past east of **La Catedral** (Wp.12) and our path starts a gentle ascent then climbing with a bit more urgency on this long slogging ascent, so pace yourself. There used to be several routes up, but now the park authorities are keeping the main *camino* immaculately clear to make the main trail more than obvious. This leads us to the saddle (Wp.13 59M) where we go a little further right (W) to the *mirador* (Wp.14) by a 'mosaic' rock outcrop overlooking the **Ucanca** plain.

Coming back from the *mirador*, all that is left is the mercilessly steep ascent (E) along the grit covered path back to our starting point. Voices come down to us from above - not a holy experience, but crowds of package tourists released from their coaches line the **Mirador de la Ruleta** above us. Climbing the most energetic section of our route under their watchful eye is rather unnerving, so it's a bit of a disappointment not to be cheered as we spring over the parapet onto the *mirador* (Wp.15 75M).

Paisaje Lunar's unique 'moonscape' geology is one of Tenerife's classic routes which should be on all walkers 'must do' list. The basic route (B) is a straightforward climb to **Paisaje Lunar**, from where we take an eastern return route via **Campamento Madre del Agua** revealing a more varied landscape (two hours walking). There's also the option of walking in from the TF-21 junction (A) just above Km66 (6.5kms and 90 minutes each way). For walkers wanting a full day in the heights above **Vilaflor**, we include a brief description of the **Agua Agria** *pista forestal* (C) which takes in unusual rock formations and the spectacularly sited 'dead tree' *mirador*. There's a short vertiginous section between Wps.14 and 15.

The refurbished **Pista Madre del Agua** provides a slightly rough but popular driving (20km/h speed limit) access to our 'official' start at Wp.9. Note: Hire car insurance only covers driving on tarmac roads! Park responsibly as this is technically a public road. The vehicle barrier, just off the TF-21, is unlocked as we go to press but may be subject to closure by the forestry authority.

(A) From TF-21 and return, 4 walker; *(B)* basic circular walk (Wps.9-27), 3 walker; *(C)* TF-21 to **Paisaje Lunar** and **Pista Agua Agria**, 5 walker

Access by car: if the **Pista Madre del Agua** vehicle barrier is closed, the nearest parking is at **Mirador Pino Gordo** (Big Pine), 1.2km down the TF-21, opposite the forestry house above **Vilaflor**; see map section.

(A) From Pista Madre del Agua to the start of the main walk

We start from just past Km66 on the TF-21 where we turn off at the hairpin bend onto a broad *pista forestal* (Wp.1). Setting the odometer to zero, we set off along the dirt road, passing a path off to the left and a chained private *pista* to the right, then a ruined cottage on our left at 2.4km (Wp.2). We pass the barred *pista* to **Galería El Pino** at 3.2km (Wp.3) after which we go downhill to cross the watercourse of **Barranco de la Mesa** shortly after which the **GR131** crosses the *pista* (Wp.4); here we have an option to follow the new trail, as an alternative to walking along the *pista*, to arrive at Wp.10. Now we are climbing the eastern valley wall to pass a ruined cottage on our left (Wp.5) at 4.4km. Then it's back to easy strolling, or driving, to pass a forest track crossing the *pista*, 4.7km, just before coming to a junction at 4.8km (Wp.6); 'Agua Agria' is signed up to the left as we continue front right on the main *pista*, signed 'Barranco del Río (*sin salida*)'.

We cross the **Granadilla** boundary at 5.1km and a *pista* off to our left, 5.3km (Wp.7) signed 'Agua Agria', the route of our *Option (C)*. A forest trail is passed at 5.6km just before a major junction, 5.8km (Wp.8), where a broad trail goes left and then a *pista* runs off right. Past another chained *pista* off to our right, 6.1km, we reach the start of car parking along the side of the track and the path junction, 6.5km (Wp.9), for the 'official' start of the **Paisaje Lunar** walking route.

(B) Main Walk

At the start of the path (Wp.9 0M) a sign informs us that 'Paisaje Lunar (Los Escurriales)' is 2.2km. We set off along the stone-lined trail through the pines to come to a cross-roads of paths (Wp.10 7M), where we join the **PR TF 72** loop trail to go right and in a couple of metres left to follow the main path steadily uphill through the young pines. Our broad trail narrows down and takes us steadily up through the woods to cross a stretch of bare lava (Wp.11 18M), then through a gate of two pines (Wp.12 33M) immediately followed by a river of lava boulders. Just after crossing a water runoff (Wp.13 39M) we come up to the lower of the two *mirador* viewpoints overlooking the **Paisaje Lunar** rockscape (Wp.14), one of the best photo opportunities on the route.

The white and beige pumice rocks appear close, but there's still a little way to go. Leaving the official **PR TF 72** trail, we pick the left of the two fainter paths, 5 metres to the left of the mapboard (N), marked 'wrong way'.

At Wp.14, leaving the PR TF 72

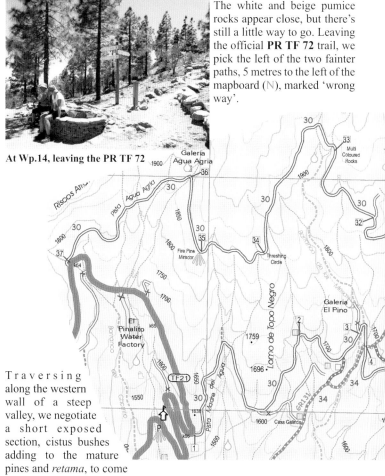

Traversing along the western wall of a steep valley, we negotiate a short exposed section, cistus bushes adding to the mature pines and *retama*, to come to the edge of the surreal lunar rockscape (Wp.15 47M), where we swing sharp right (SE) and pass below the first group of the white towers (several short paths fork left to approach the pumice surface), following metal orange waymarks.

After taking a break under a large pine, we continue down the narrow path (0M) carefully picking our way down to a watercourse to cross the ravine floor (Wp.16) before coming onto the white sand surface to pass another section of lunar rockscape.

Pumice 'towers' at Wp.15

After 30 metres the fine white pumice sand underfoot gives way to a woodland path (Wp.17) running along the eastern side of this floriferous valley, cushion-like yellow lotus plants lining our route as if deliberately planted there.

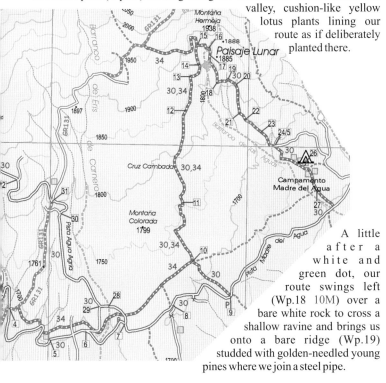

A little after a white and green dot, our route swings left (Wp.18 10M) over a bare white rock to cross a shallow ravine and brings us onto a bare ridge (Wp.19) studded with golden-needled young pines where we join a steel pipe.

Bearing right after 80 metres, we leave the steel pipe at a skew pine (Wp.20) and come onto a second bare ridge. Heading down the ridge line, we cross another steel pipe (Wp.21) on bare rock to come amongst pines, then climb up the eastern ridge to cross the spur at an orange waymark (Wp.22 22M).

We follow the path down, passing a retaining wall and crossing yet another steel pipe, 50 metres after which we bear right and down at a T-junction (Wp.23) where the barred branch straight on traverses the slope.

Campamento Madre del Agua

The sturdy chalets of **Campamento Madre del Agua** come into view across a large valley. Our path down the spur requires careful footwork, water erosion not helping as we swing left below a large pine to drop down onto a *pista* (Wp.24 34M).

20 metres down the dirt track as it curves round in a sharp U-bend we step off the track onto a trail (Wp.25) that leads down to a bare ridge studded with young pines and the first of the sturdy chalets.

Down through the encampment, we come to a cluster of picnic tables (in sight of the car park) below which we find a hut named 'Auchón' (Wp.26). To the right of its entrance door, we walk in south-easterly direction, spotting a distinct stone-lined trail in the distance after a few metres of walking.

200 metres from the hut we come to a T-junction (Wp.27, green dot on a low wall), where a broad trail continues straight on to feed onto **Pista Madre del Agua**, while the fainter path to the right shadows the dirt road to eventually join our outward route at Wp.10. Track or trail for the final section is your personal choice.

(C) Pista Agua Agria

From the junction on **Pista Madre del Agua** (Wp.7) we swing up the narrow *pista* to come up to a cute bridge over a ravine (Wp.28) before climbing up to a T-junction (Wp.29) where we go right. Now it is up through the trees, passing a *pista* off left (Wp.30) before crossing the **GR131** waymarked route (Wp.31) then 150 metres later a crude forest trail off right (Wp.32).

Now we come to the most impressive section as our track runs along the side of a very steep valley through a region of unusually coloured rocks (Wp.33). Coming back amongst the forest, we pass a strangely located threshing circle (Wp.34) and eventually climb up the rough *pista* to **Fire Pine Mirador** (Wp.35) where we can take a break accompanied by one of the south's most awesome of views.

After the *mirador* there is more rough track before we reach **Galería Agua Agria** 'sour water' (Wp.36) from where it's rough going, particularly on the descent down onto the TF-21 (Wp.37). Having walked this route so far, then we have an easy 2km stroll down the TF-21, passing the entrance to the **Fuente Alta** water factory, to the entrance to **Pista Madre del Agua** (Wp.1).

Montaña Guajara dominates the sharp escarpment which encloses the southern wall of **Las Cañadas**. Viewed from the **Parador** with sheer cliffs ringing its summit, it looks indomitable. In truth it's a straightforward if strenuous hike on our chosen route. **Guajara**'s plateau summit can be cold and windy, so take a jacket no matter how good the weather looks. On arrival in **Las Cañadas** a 10-20 minute break (**Parador Café** if open) is recommended to enable acclimatisation to the altitude. A visit to the adjacent **National Park Tourist Office** to check the status of trails is also worth while.

In June 2016, the park authorities opened a new trail connecting **Guajara** with **Degollada de Ucanca**, making for an attractive circular route along official paths. We have replaced our old descent which followed the exposed northern face, now officially prohibited. Archaeologists and ancient-cultures enthusiasts may find exciting a possibility to 'travel back in time' on this route. A short distance before reaching **Degollada de Ucanca** (Wps.20-21), we found traces of ceramics and primitive cutting tools made of obsidian, well over 500-years-old remains of Guanches, the aborigine inhabitants of the island, who were seasonally coming from the lowlands and across the **Ucanca** pass to seek pastures for their herds.

Mouflon restrictions: Due to mouflon control, this route is <u>closed</u> when the restrictions are in place. See page 10 for details.

5 | 3¾ H | 10.5 km | 630m / 630m | ↻ | 1*

* Parador Café

Access by bus: N°342 from **Playa de las Américas** & **Los Cristianos**, N°348 from **Puerto de la Cruz**; there is only one departure and return of these routes each day, so make sure you don't miss your bus!

Access by car: The park authorities have closed off access to the dirt *pistas* such as **Siete Cañadas** which used to provide a lot of car parking, thus putting increased pressure on the **Mirador de la Ruleta** car park and the limited amount of road side parking near the **Parador Café**.

Degollada de Ucanca visible after Wp.2

From just south of the **Parador** and next to the **Tourist Office** on the corner, we pass a notice board (Wp.1) to step onto a narrow trail (SSE) heading down across the *malpaís*. Our trail brings us down onto the **Siete Cañadas** *pista* (Wp.2 9M) where we turn left to pass a black-stone hut (Wp.3 10M) immediately followed by the vehicle barrier to continue along the dirt road. We pass the yellow **Piedra Amarilla** rocks until, as the *pista* comes up to take a long climbing loop, we have a chance to step off onto a narrow trail (Wp.4 22M). A steady zig-zagging climb brings us back onto the **Pista Siete**

Cañadas (Wp.5 27M) to be rewarded with a downhill stroll past the **Sanatorium** track on our left (Wp.6 38M). 5 minutes later we come to a junction, where we join the main section of the **GR131** (Wp.7 43M).

Leaving the *pista*, we follow the **GR131** trail (SE) in a steady climb with the yellow-lichened cliffs of **Guajara** above us on our right. We climb in lazy zig-zags, pushing our way through Teide broom, which threatens to take over our route in places. At over 2200 metres altitude this feels like a major climb as we toil relentlessly upwards.

Our reward comes as we crest the ridge onto the **Degollada de Guajara** (Wp.8 70M). The saddle provides us with magnificent views over **Las Cañadas** to the north and down the **Barranco del Río** to the south, plus some comfortable rocks to sit on while taking a break.

The **PR TF 86** goes left to **Villa de Arico** while we continue (0M) along the **GR131** to the right (SW), ignoring an immediate right branch. A short descent brings us under white pumice cliffs before our path starts climbing up through a tumble of rocks to the **Guajara** junction (Wp.9 8M) marked by a National Park's route **Nº15** noticeboard. Ahead, the **GR131** running down a black *picón* ridge towards **Paisaje Lunar** is visible, while we turn right (W) to start the long ascent to the summit of **Guajara**. Our well-trodden path climbs steadily, snaking gently among shrubs of *retama* to come over a short section of a bare rock (Wp.10 18M), just before passing a pinnacle on our left. Crossing then re-crossing a watercourse, our white-and-mauve *picón* path runs across boulders (Wp.11 21M) before a short section of log steps (Wp.12 24M) eases our climb on at-times-slippery fine gravel. We pass a rocky outcrop (Wp.13 32M), after which the path straightens out for several hundred metres.

Wp.15, the summit junction

It takes us up to cross a stone-paved watercourse, after which we negotiate a set of log steps (Wp.14 41M), before the trail winds around a corner into tall shrubs of *retama*. The clearly defined trail then runs in a trench-like cutting, snaking steadily up and further up to come to a signposted junction (Wp.15 50M), where the *retama* gives

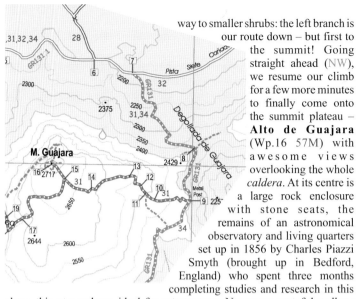

way to smaller shrubs: the left branch is our route down – but first to the summit! Going straight ahead (NW), we resume our climb for a few more minutes to finally come onto the summit plateau – **Alto de Guajara** (Wp.16 57M) with awesome views overlooking the whole *caldera*. At its centre is a large rock enclosure with stone seats, the remains of an astronomical observatory and living quarters set up in 1856 by Charles Piazzi Smyth (brought up in Bedford, England) who spent three months completing studies and research in this clean, thin atmosphere, ideal for astronomers. Numerous grateful walkers now find the rock remains useful as windbreaks on this exposed plateau.

The old unofficial path to **Degollada de Ucanca** follows a northerly direction from the summit toward a trig point located on a promontory visible below us; this route is now officially banned. We retrace our steps (0M) back to Wp.15 (4M), where we turn right (S). Our comfortable path turns west as we descend across the sloping plain, before it swings left to traverse a ravine. Below us, a massive rock fissure comes into our view. The trail takes us down to this huge cleft through a series of tight switchbacks on quite slippery *picón*, before we join the rock face on our left (Wp.17 22M) to continue directly under the sheer cliffs (risk of rock fall). Views of **Degollada de Ucanca**, **Parador** and **Teide** open up as we walk through the fissure.

Leaving the cliffs, the path swings north towards **Teide** to pass a lone juniper (Wp.18 30M). After the steep descent we now traverse a slope of shrubs and cross over a clump of boulders (Wp.19 34M), before coming to a signpost (Wp.20 42M). We turn (SW) sharp left (the branch from the right is the exposed old path from **Guajara**). A few minutes later we emerge from the shrubs into the open and passing a giant boulder stroll onto the **Degollada de Ucanca** (Wp.21 50M), a crossroads with a cluster of signposts.

From the *degollada* a clear path drops down (NW) until it swings sharp right (Wp.22 52M) for us to descend on a tricky rock shale surface below a north facing cliff. Carefully picking our footsteps we move out from the cliffs onto the 'Thousand ZigZags' descent, passing above a nice rock tower (Wp.23 63M) on our left and coming down through more twists and turns before our route straightens out to pass a solitary pine (Wp.24 73M). We then come onto a small saddle (Wp.25 77M) in front of a multi-coloured peak, from where our path swings right (NE) to bring us onto a manicured yellow rock path. Our trail brings us along to cross the water runoff beside the **Pista Siete Cañadas** (Wp.2) which we cross over onto the trail to walk across the *malpaís* back to the **Parador** (Wp.1).

32

Siete Cañadas, one of Tenerife's most popular high altitude walking routes, is so easy to navigate that a description of the route could be: 'Start on the dirt road opposite **El Portillo Visitors' Centre**. Walk along the dirt road until reaching a vehicle barrier and a black-stone hut and then turn right for the **Parador**.' and there you have it!

Of course, there's much more to the route than that. The sheer scale of **Las Cañadas** with its distant panorama can be daunting. Then it's approx 2,000 metres altitude, with thin air. That said, it's a 'must do' route for fit walkers. One tip is to check the wind direction and walk downwind. Go prepared for the desert with full sun protection of hat, sunglasses, high factor sun cream, adequate clothing and footwear, plenty (2+ litres) of water plus snacks. Before tackling this walk, you should have experienced shorter routes at this altitude to check your tolerance.

Mouflon restrictions: Due to mouflon control, this route is <u>closed</u> when the restrictions are in place. See page 10 for details.

* at the Parador Café

Access by bus: Nº342 from **Playa de las Américas** to **El Portillo Visitors' Centre**, return from the **Parador**. Nº348 from **Puerto de la Cruz** to **El Portillo Visitors' Centre**, return from the **Parador**. Note that the 348 allows approximately 45 minutes more walking time between arrival and departure times.

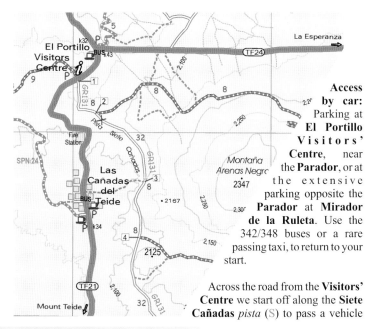

Access by car: Parking at **El Portillo Visitors' Centre**, near the **Parador**, or at the extensive parking opposite the **Parador** at **Mirador de la Ruleta**. Use the 342/348 buses or a rare passing taxi, to return to your start.

Across the road from the **Visitors' Centre** we start off along the **Siete Cañadas** *pista* (S) to pass a vehicle

Wp.3 - El Portillo path

barrier (Wp.1 0M), strolling downhill and then up to where our 'Arenas Negras' trail leaves the dirt road (Wp.2 8M) just after which we pass another metal barrier; even this little section is rather enervating in the thin atmosphere. We've under four and a half hours to get to the **Parador** if we're to catch our bus back down the mountain; we'll have to walk at a fair lick with minimal stops. Our GPS shows that we are walking through the broken hills at this end of **Las Cañadas** at 5km/h. Allowing for the stops to drink from our water bottles and a couple of short rests, we should just make it in time for the bus.

Passing a path off to our right to **El Portillo Alto** (Wp.3 20M), we come out of the floriferous foothills into the crater proper. The huge vista unrolls before us, the **Pista Siete Cañadas** winding its way across the crater floor until it disappears as a pinpoint in the far distance. The vastness of what we have to cover is daunting to say the least - the landscape's sheer immensity takes your breath away.

After passing the second **Arenas Negras** junction (Wp.4 24M) we really are on our own and while our GPS shows that we're still walking at 5km/h, our progress across the vastness is imperceptible. It's only by stopping and looking back along the *pista* do we get any impression of how much progress we've made.

Wp.4, the 2nd Arenas Negras junction

The geological landscape is remarkable. One of the surprises is, that while we may think of volcanic crater floors as being flat, this one certainly is not. Fifty-metre drops into lava sand basins open up beside our route and wind-eroded rocks loom over the dirt road, framing cliffs in the crater rim (Wp.5 36M). After skirting a lava ridge, the bulk of **Montaña Guajara** comes into view in the far distance; when we finally pass below its cliffs we'll be within an hour of finishing, but that moment is still a long way away.

Eventually we come along past a remote weather sensor to curve around a giant rock hand at the end of a promontory thrust out from the crater rim (Wp.6 67M). This feature is important not so much for its remarkable geology but for walkers' sanity, as without these markers this route could easily devolve into that nightmare scenario where no matter how hard you try you just can't make progress; the challenge of this route is both physical and psychological.

Three minutes later we pass a right hand fork leading to **Minas de San José**. Gaudiesque rock structures are passed before a seat-sized rock beside the *pista* tempts us into taking a break (Wp.7 82M). One of the best feelings you get from hard walking is when you stop doing it! It's just so good to sit down that you just want to keep on doing it. Mountain walkers know the pure pleasure that comes from having a 'good sit down', even on a sharp rock.

Levering ourselves back onto the dirt road we push along at our regulatory 5km/h, passing interesting cubes of rock (Wp.8 93M), looking as if they've been sculpted but more likely to be unusual 'volcanic bombs' dropped here during the crater's formation. We slog up a rise (Wp.9 105M) to pass a pre-shattered promontory thrust out from the rim, a scree of rock cubes showing the results of previous weathering. We are buoyed by the sight of **Guajara** coming back into view, much closer now but still a few kilometres away as we pass beneath an impressive peak in the crater rim (Wp.10 134M) above a pumice cliff.

A steady downhill slope takes us past the remains of the shepherds' huts (Wp.11 139M), unused since grazing was banned in the crater, followed by an easy stretch of the *pista* across a sea of lava grit; on our left is an amazing display of *tajinastes* at the foot of the crater rim and higher up amongst the peaks.

This easy stretch runs out as the road swings up to cross a lava ridge in the steepest ascent yet. Down on the coast this would be enough of a 'grinding' climb but up here in the thin air, it's hard work. A shattered 'hog's back' rock beside the *pista* gives an excuse to stop for a photo and then it's off again until we pass an interesting rock cone (Wp.12 180M) with an eroded rock wall alongside it where thankfully, the climbing ends.

We're keeping up to our 4-5km/h walking speed schedule as we sweep down towards the base of **Guajara** before another upward slope brings us to the junction with our 'Mighty Guajara' route (Wp.13 195M), where we take a couple of minutes break before tackling another slogging slope ahead to round an impressively shattered promontory.

We manage a spring in our step as we come along to the **Sanatorium** track junction (Wp.14 201M) of our 'Montaña Majúa - Toffee Mountain' route, the ghostly remains of the scattered buildings hidden from view. Now we sweep down between craggy shattered summits and the lava flow wall to come to a discreet walking trail on our left near a metal cover (Wp.15 214M) whose picky descent cuts off a long loop of the *pista*.

Back on the dirt road (Wp.16 219M) we sweep down to a view over the **Parador**, where in the left turn of the road a shortcut path (Wp.17 227M) descends down the lava crest, joining the trail below us that we will take across the *malpaís* to the hotel.

Piedras Amarillas backed by Guajara (Wps.16-17)

For a more comfortable and gentler descent, we follow the long loop of the dirt road down past a vehicle barrier and rangers' hut (Wp.18) before reaching a crossroads with a trail (Wp.19 232M).

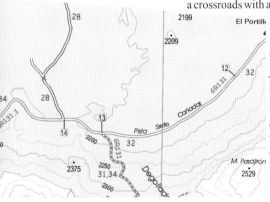

Turning right, our trail is joined by the shortcut path (Wp.20 235M) where the main trail turns away from the lava crest, before it twists and turns through the *malpaís* towards the **Parador**.

We're going to finish before the bus departure time - we could even have time for a drink in the café, so we press on to reach the signboard (Wp.21) at the trail's end, exactly four hours after setting out from the **Visitors' Centre**.

33

"That looks a bit of a challenge", we said while studying the old military maps and, "It doesn't appear in anybody else's guide book", as we discussed researching a walk from the **Parador** down to **Vilaflor**. Being familiar with the **Degollada de Ucanca** on the crater rim and knowing of the *camino* down from **Las Lajas** to **Vilaflor**, all we had to do was link the two sections. Sounds simple? The plan was, bus to the **Parador** on the N°342, walk the crater rim, possibly taking in **Sombrero de Chasna** before descending to **Las Lajas** followed by an easy descent to **Vilaflor** where we'd catch the last N°482 bus for **Los Cristianos**. That's 6½ hours if you're to catch the bus; we missed it by a margin, but hampered by broken footwear (Ros), shale covered downhill trails (our least favourite surface), and an attack of vertigo (David). If you're fit and quick you should make it well in time for the last bus, though it's not for nothing that this route is called 'The Big One' - it's a challenge route only to be undertaken in good weather.

Looking back at Teide after Wp.3

Mouflon restrictions: Due to mouflon control this route is <u>closed</u> when the restrictions are in place. See page 10 for details.

Access by bus: N°342 from **Playa de Las Américas/Los Cristianos**. Return by N°482 from **Vilaflor** for **Los Cristianos** (weekends & fiestas only); otherwise N°474 from **Vilaflor** (working days only) to **Arona** then change to N°480 to **Los Cristianos**.

Access by car: if you don't want to risk missing the last bus then you could drive to **Vilaflor** ahead of the N°342, park and bus to the **Parador**.

NB After the spectacular drive up to the **Parador**, take a few minutes acclimatising to the thin atmosphere before setting off.

We start from the notice board on the southern side of the **Parador** (Wp.1 0M) on the narrow trail heading across the *malpaís* to cross the **Siete Cañadas** track (Wp.2 11M) onto trail **Nº31** 'Cumbres de Ucanca' which we follow to head towards the crater rim. Our stone-littered path winds through the *malpaís*, then starts climbing.

At Wp.2, views of our objective, Degollada de Ucanca

A steady ascent in the thin air brings us onto a saddle (Wp.3) before we labour up through the zigzags and pass under a cliff to enjoy the expanding views before finally reaching the top of our ascent (Wp.4 69M) to come onto the rim at the **Degollada de Ucanca**, a good place to take a break.

We set off from the crossroads of trails on the *degollada* along the right-hand path (0M SW). There have been plenty of walkers before us leading to a confusion of paths in places, while other sections are refreshingly clear; no matter, the views are stupendous especially to the south. Alongside the path is a waymarked rock (Wp.5) as we head steadily west to encounter a scrambly ascent (Wp.6 8M) to pass through rock outcrops.

Our path brings us up onto the actual crater rim for more stupendous views, then becomes more difficult in a picky descent alongside dramatic drops to the **Ucanca** plain three hundred metres below. Our route turns away from the rim to negotiate the southern slopes of a rock outcrop (Wp.7 18M), then we're ascending again onto a broad *lomo* giving extensive views (Wp.8 32M). We drop down to a saddle then up onto the crater rim to an area of great rock footballs (Wp.9 44M) which make convenient seats before tackling the next slope and a clambering ascent, guided by green dots, through large broken rocks (Wp.10 60M) to come under the cliff wall for another tricky section of the path. It's a wild mountain route, almost pathless below the cliffs, before climbing up through the rocks to a cairn (Wp.11 72M). Guided by a second cairn, we continue west, a path emerging as we ascend through Teide broom to pass a volcanic 'bomb' (Wp.12 76M). Our route is confirmed by a green dot on a smaller bomb as we stroll through the broom in an 'upland plateau' landscape, stepping through an old wall and visiting the rim again before coming onto a miscellany of rocks. Green dots and cairns mark a route over the rocks heading towards a white dot and arrow in the middle distance. Passing the white arrow (Wp.13 85M) we come up to views down over *tajinaste*-dotted slopes to **Vilaflor** in the far distance. Past the white dot, we climb over a rock outcrop, then down and scrambling up again, this 'up and down' repeated as we follow white dot waymarking along the crater rim (Wp.14 100M) to edge towards **Sombrero de Chasna**. Finally we come onto a boulder outcrop (Wp.15 106M) with a white waymark fifty metres ahead.

Timings, realistic to this point, become a little surreal as David suffers a little vertigo moment. To reach the waymark involves lowering yourself onto a narrow rock shelf that overhangs the drop into the crater, edging across the shelf and then back up onto the rim. We look at it, then pick our way amongst the boulders looking for an easier way, which there isn't, so we take a break to consider the matter.

Beyond the boulder massif where we're seated we can see a clear path, and the thought of giving up and making the three-hour slog back to the **Parador** is marginally less appealing than dangling over a thousand-foot drop. Ros drops down onto the shelf and skips across to the white waymark, while David's traverse is somewhat slower before clearing the six-foot shelf (0M).

Off the rock, we have the luxury of a path, then at a T-junction (Wp.16) a path literally drops into the crater as we go left on a steady descent through broom to come onto a clear path that climbs to reach a crest on the crater rim. Now it's downhill to a path junction (Wp.17), where we bear left shortly before a second junction marked by

At the rim near Wp.17

a large waymarked rock (Wp.18 9M) where we choose the downwards option towards **Sombrero de Chasna** and descend to another junction at two big cairns (Wp.19 13M) where a path heads up the peak's gentle eastern flank for those who wish to take in views from on top of the 'Hat' (See Walk 18).

We head right, down the valley between **Sombrero de Chasna** and the rim, the shale-covered trail making for a picky descent alongside the watercourse to pass a 'mushroom' rock before coming to a path junction (Wp.20 29M) where we go left to a large boulder, our path even more 'rubble-ised' until we cross the watercourse a second time (Wp.21 35M) 50 metres after which we bear left at a Y-junction, where Walk 18 goes right.

Great rock buttresses punctuate the pine-clothed slopes which roll out into views over the south coast as we descend through the trees, unfortunately loose shale again covering the trail, so it's back to a slow picky descent on the serpentine path. Down below a large rock pillar we come to a path junction (Wp.22 52M), an arrow pointing back the way we've come; we keep to the picky path on the right of the watercourse, more shale slope than path, to come down to a large rock with a white dot waymark (Wp.23 55M) followed by a plethora of mini-cairns guiding us down through the forest. Our cairn-marked route contours along past a white arrow on a rock (Wp.24 74M), then a skittery descent brings us onto a path for a gentle ascent onto a broad *lomo*. From its crest we sight tarmac through the trees; after so long in the 'wilderness' it's a reassuring sight. A steady, picky descent sees Walk 18 join us from the right (Wp.25 86M) from here we follow the route of Walk 18 to come to the TF-21 road (Wp.26 92M).

We go through the tunnel to use the cross-country route (Walk 18) to the **Las Lajas** recreation area, to stroll down to the picnic tables (Wp.27 118M). After three hours on our feet negotiating some of the picky-est trails we've known, it would be an act of madness to turn down the opportunity for a sit down.

Tired but refreshed, we head down to the football pitch where we find the signboard (Wp.28 0M) at the start of our final trail; 'Camino Las Lajas San Roque' 6.25 kilometres, descent 600 metres, Time 4 hours (!), Average Difficulty'.

Signboards lead us to expect nice manicured paths and this one starts quite well as it drops down into a valley before curving around **Montaña Las Lajas** with panoramic views of the south-west. The *camino* is organised as a set of information points and after a steady uphill we arrive at 'Paradores Pasteleras' (Wp.29 13M), then curve up around the mountain to 'Campo de Volcanes de Ifonche' (Wp.30 21M) with its battered signboard. Our path now starts a steady descent through Canarian pines and pink cistus, unfortunately rock-littered and water-eroded making for another slow picky descent to a multi-trunked fire-blackened pine (Wp.31 32M) before crossing a polished boulder watercourse (Wp.32 36M). Over the watercourse, our path is just as bad as we pick our way down to overlook a proper *barranco* (Wp.33 57M) into which we begin to drop. A massively rock-stepped section take us down to cross the watercourse (Wp.34 69M); on the left bank a proper path takes us zigzagging up before contouring along above the deepening ravine with impressive buttress walls, to 'Basaltos Antiguos' (Wp.35 78M), some of the oldest rocks in Tenerife. Crossing a watercourse of the *barranco*, a short climb brings us into an open landscape of gentle rock slopes dotted with pines and cistus. After passing a walled pine we cross a dirt *pista* (Wp.36 92M), a picky path then bringing us back onto it (Wp.37 95M).

The *pista* becomes more water-eroded as we follow it downhill, passing above a water hut. A big green arrow directs us across a watercourse (Wp.38 100M) to continue up a rough path which levels out and improves shortly before 'El Pinar' (Wp.39 105M), then reverts to its rough nature, at least with panoramic views of the south coast. We descend to cross a watercourse before meeting concrete covered water pipes running alongside our route (Wp.40 114M) which provide comfortable seating.

Ros is wearing her toughest 'hard rock' mountain walking sandals which choose this point to shed an ankle strap. A rough repair means our timings are even slower as we descend from a rock outcrop to cross a *barranco* watercourse (Wp.41 127M), more water pipes coming together in the valley, then coming to 'Eres' (Wp.42 130M) with its battered signboard. Green dot waymarks lead us across rough rocks, then we cross another watercourse alongside steel water pipes (Wp.43 136M). Green dots take us downhill to re-cross the water pipe on the roughest of paths which becomes easier after we meet the **GR131**. We arrive at a water junction (Wp.44 147M) to catch a glimpse of our first house, which resolves itself into the pumping house of a roofed *embalse* as we descend the crude track to a crossroads of *pistas* set on a saddle (Wp.45 153M). Swinging left, we follow a green arrow (E) down a *pista* into a terraced valley of vines to pass two access tracks (Wps.46 & 47) before dropping down to civilisation in the form of the football ground and a tarmac road (Wp.48 161M).

After those rough trails the tarmac provides luxury strolling as we pass the impressive **Hotel Villalba** to a junction where the main street swings left (**GR131**) for an alternative finish in upper **Vilaflor**; we keep straight ahead on the minor lane which descends past the cemetery on our left and a home observatory on our right, the street dropping steeply as it becomes lined with houses, so steep that it would benefit from being staired. We skitter down through a sharp bend to drop onto the main road (Wp.49 171M), the street appropriately named **Calle la Ladera** - literally 'Ladder Street'! We're way past the last bus departure but if you've kept going and avoided accidents then you will have an easy stroll down the road, to the **Vilafor** bus stop at the petrol station, well in time for your bus connection.

Paisaje Lunar (**Lunar Landscape**) is one of Tenerife's most popular walking destinations for which we offer a dedicated walking route, Walk 30, so why another new route? Well, our car-based Walk 30 isn't practical for bus users, while this route can be done using Titsa buses.

Trails led down from the **Degollada de Ucanca** and **Degollada de Guajara** before the **GR131** was created so, looking for a top range day-hike, we've combined our trails with the (then) opened **Vilaflor** *sendero* (now part of the **GR131**) for a classic adventure. This is a 'big dayout' adventure at altitude, equally spectacular as 'Crater Rim Challenge', perhaps even more colourful in terms of landscape diversity though not as challenging. If you can handle the 300 metre ascent to the **Degollada de Guajara** in the thin air (2,000+ metres altitude) you'll enjoy this long linear route giving a new view into **Paisaje Lunar** only seen by walkers using this route. Five walker rating is due to the altitude, ascents and distance.

Mouflon restrictions: Due to mouflon control, this route is <u>closed</u> when the restrictions are in place. See page 10 for details.

5   4½ H   16.5 km   450m / 1150m   one way   2*

* at start and end

Access by bus: Nº342 from **Playa de las Américas/Los Cristianos** to **Parador**, Nº482 from **Vilaflor** back to resorts (weekends & public holidays only). Otherwise bus Nº474 from **Vilaflor** (working days only) to **Arona**, then change to 480 for **Los Cristianos**.

Access by car: car drivers could drive to **Vilaflor** and catch the 342 from there.

On arriving at the **Parador**, it's a good idea to take a 10 minute break to let your body acclimatise to the thin atmosphere at 2,000+ metres altitude, possibly running the gauntlet of the self-service café, or simply sitting on their outside terrace.

The start of our route is the same as for Walk 31 'Mighty Guajara' (Wps.1 to 9 78M). Where 'Mighty Guajara' goes right (Wp.9 78M), we continue straight

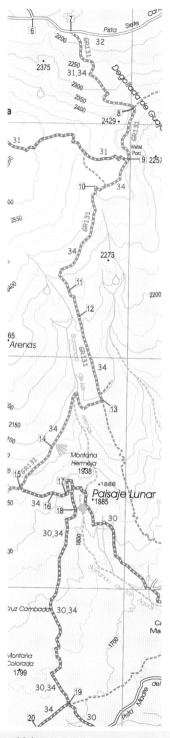

ahead on the **GR131** trail on a mixture of rock and dirt as we head SW. After turning into a small *barranco* to cross its watercourse (Wp.10) our route heads (S) in a gentle downhill descent. We come down to an old, almost hollow, pine (Wp.11 110M) while ahead we have a magnificent vista of the black and gold *picón* sand slopes of **Montaña Las Arenas**, and below us the unexpected sight of a pristine stone-lined trail heading across the black *picón* sand of a broad ridge top plain to a junction in the distance.

The *picón* trail (Wps.12-13)

A picky descent brings us onto the start of this unexpected black *picón* trail (Wp.12 118M), neatly stone-lined, where at last we can stretch our legs at proper hiking speed before coming to a major junction (Wp.13 130M) 200 metres before the forest line. Straight on would take us to the east of the camping site, a long way from where we want to be. We go right (**GR131**) on the better-walked path lined by stumpy posts before we drop off the *picón* ridge into a rock and *picón* *barranco*. A narrow trail takes us down across the ravine watercourse to face a steep *picón* ascent. We slog up over the grit to the summit where our trail continues to a small *mirador* overlooking **Paisaje Lunar** (Wp.14); this elevated *mirador* is one of the best viewpoints from which to take in the unique wind-sculpted white rock landscape.

At the *mirador* a very steep *picón* scree heads directly for the famous rock landscape. Zig-zagging down the forty-five degree scree in a slalom descent is an exciting but potentially dangerous short cut! We continue down the **GR131** trail to a junction where we meet the **PR TF 72** loop trail (Wp.15 152M). Our route goes left (ESE) while staying on the **GR131** would eventually bring you back onto our route at Wp.24, but you would miss the opportunity to explore **Paisaje Lunar**.

Views of Paisaje Lunar en route

Taking the left-hand trail (ESE) we wind steeply down the wooded slope to cross a watercourse (Wp.16) after which the gradient eases for us to come to the first of the two close-range viewpoints of **Paisaje Lunar** (Wp.17 163M). Resuming our descent (S) we cross an old concrete canal half-way to the lower of the two **Paisaje Lunar** *miradors* with a neat semi-circular stone bench (Wp.18 168M). If you want to explore the pumice towers from close up, take the narrow path to the left of the notice board (N). It traverses the steep escarpment (one short vertiginous stretch) and descends to the valley of **Paisaje Lunar** (5 mins. one way; not part of our route and times).

From the bench *mirador* (0M), we follow the **PR TF 72** trail down across a 'river' of lava boulders before passing through a gate of two pines. Our trail widens to a track before being joined by a path from our left just after which we come to a signed crossroads (Wp.19 30M).

We follow the 'Vilaflor 4.7km' sign on a beautifully made *sendero* broad enough to walk comfortably abreast as we join a dry-stone wall to a T-junction (Wp.20), where we continue straight on.

Our trail undulates through the forest to pass an S-shaped wall just before crossing the **Pista Agua Agria** (Wp.21) then the second **Agua Agria** access track (Wp.22), where we are just a touch away from the main dirt road, **Pista Madre del Agua** on our left. Passing a ruined cottage on our left, we meet the **Pista Madre del Agua** for a few metres before our *sendero* climbs away into the woods again (Wp.23) to cross a ridge where we pass another S-shaped wall to come to a junction (Wp.24) with the **GR131**. Going downhill, we drop steeply onto the **Pista Madre del Agua** at a stone-walled *sendero* entrance (Wp.25 65M), walls of a convenient height for us to take a seat enjoying the views. Across the *pista*, we follow the **GR131** that continues seductively down into the *barranco*. After dropping steeply down past a large retaining

Past a ruined cottage (Wps.22-23)

wall to the watercourse, the *sendero* then climbs steeply up the western wall of the *barranco* to reach a trail junction at its summit (Wp.27). Alternatively, we can avoid this descent/ascent by going right along the **Pista Madre del Agua**, to cross the

barranco for a gentle climb up to a large pine. Here, a green spot (Wp.26) guides us off the *pista* onto a very faint trail which takes us down to pass to the left of an *embalse*, after which we briefly join a beekeepers' track before rejoining the GR route at the junction (Wp.27 75M).

Wp.25; cross or follow Pista Madre del Agua

Now it is down again as the **GR131** follows an old donkey trail down towards **Vilaflor** and while it is broad, it is also a very picky, knee-jarringly slow descent. **Vilaflor** looks tantalisingly close as we pick our way down the trail to pass a left-hand trail signed 'Circuito de Atletismo de Montaña' before coming down between terraces onto a *pista* (Wp.28 99M) below the village. Here we turn left to cross the *barranco* watercourse, a steady climb up the trail onto a paved driveway brings us to the first of the village houses (Wp.29).

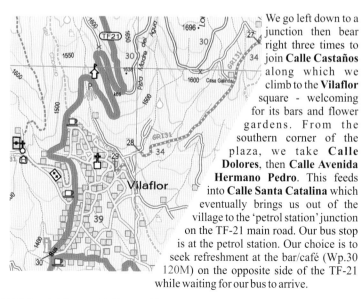

We go left down to a junction then bear right three times to join **Calle Castaños** along which we climb to the **Vilaflor** square - welcoming for its bars and flower gardens. From the southern corner of the plaza, we take **Calle Dolores**, then **Calle Avenida Hermano Pedro**. This feeds into **Calle Santa Catalina** which eventually brings us out of the village to the 'petrol station' junction on the TF-21 main road. Our bus stop is at the petrol station. Our choice is to seek refreshment at the bar/café (Wp.30 120M) on the opposite side of the TF-21 while waiting for our bus to arrive.

Mount Teide isn't a big mountain, it's a VERY BIG mountain; at 3,718 metres altitude, it's the highest point in Spain and you would need to travel a long way to find anything this big. We make this point because many people/walkers have the impression that it is an easy walk; straightforward maybe, but easy, NO. **Teide** is difficult for two reasons:-

1) You MUST have an official permit to get to the summit. You can get your *permiso* free of charge online at www.reservasparquesnacionales.es and print it out. Everyone in your group must bring ID. Only 160 people per day divided into 4 two-hour time slots are allowed on the peak, so choose your slot to suit your party assuming there are any vacancies on the day you plan to climb. Permits are often booked out weeks in advance. If you come to Tenerife without a permit there's still a chance for you to make it. Those staying at the **Refugio de Altavista** (3260m) get the permit automatically, provided they climb onto the summit for the sunrise, a common practice from the *refugio*.

2) Thinner air means less oxygen for each lungful of air you breathe in. At these altitudes that's 50% of the oxygen you get at sea level. Climbing 200 metres from the cable car to the peak is tough going, while the 1,350 metres ascent up the **Montaña Blanca** track requires an extreme level of fitness.

The *teleférico* is a wonderful method of ascending 1,200 metres at these altitudes so this is how Joe and myself tackled the mountain on our 'Boy's Adventure' day out. Then just as we were about to publish the park authorities opened their new **SPN39** (trail **Nº39**) official trail linking the **Montaña Blanca** track with the **Sanatorio** track to make a circular walking route the new prefered option.

* 10kms for bus users finishing the hike at Wp.17.
   14kms for car drivers using the SPN39 trail (**Nº39**) circular option; 4.8hrs, circular.
   18kms for the classic (out & back) ascent/descent fromWp.17; 7hrs, out & back.
** Cable-car station cafe and **Altavista** refuge vending machines.

Access by bus: Nº342 from **Playa de las Américas** & **Los Cristianos**, Nº348 from **Puerto de la Cruz**; there's only one departure and return service each day. The cable-car station and Km40.6 of the TF-21are official bus stops.

Access by car: with the opening of the **SPN39** (*sendero* **Nº39**) hiking trail that links the teleferico station road with the **Montaña Blanca** track we have a circular 'cable car up, walk down' route; so park at either the cable-car station or opposite the end of the **Montaña Blanca** track (Km40,6 of the TF-21).

Waiting for the cable car to arrive should give you ten minutes acclimatising to the altitude. The *teleférico* operators ensure the cars are packed to capacity making for an intimate ascent. Once out of the terminus there is a viewing area, a good place for acclimatising to the higher altitude for another ten minutes while enjoying the views before setting off on our climb.

From the cable-car terminus (Wp.1), we recommend the 700-metre stroll (W) to the **Mirador de Pico Viejo** (Wp.2), overlooking a fascinating crater of the 'Old Peak', whose view is obstructed from **Teide**'s summit. **Pico Viejo** has the biggest and one of the most beautiful and complete craters on the island, especially enjoyable from this altitude and angle (about 15 mins one-way, not counted in our total timing). This short stroll can also help you adapt to the altitude before tackling the summit.

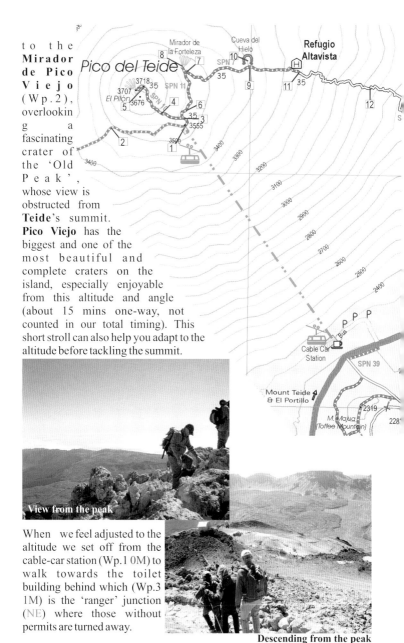

View from the peak

When we feel adjusted to the altitude we set off from the cable-car station (Wp.1 0M) to walk towards the toilet building behind which (Wp.3 1M) is the 'ranger' junction (NE) where those without permits are turned away.

Descending from the peak

Two rangers check our *permiso* in detail against our identification (all your party must pass onto the restricted peak en-bloc), before we're allowed to start climbing the well-made rock trail that leads up to the peak towering over us. It's a busy trail even though limited to those with permits, so you'll get to meet plenty of other 'peak hikers' as parties leapfrog each other, then taking rest stops, of which we take a number before reaching a *mirador* viewpoint turn in the trail (Wp.4). It's a well-made trail, a straightforward ascent except that at

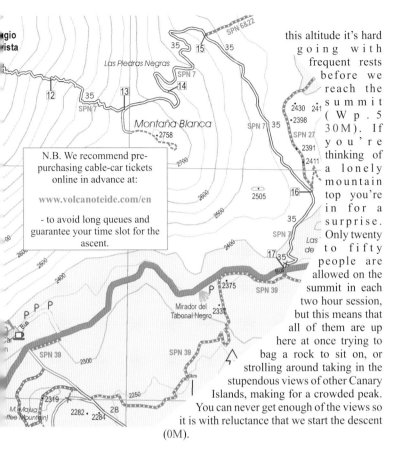

this altitude it's hard going with frequent rests before we reach the summit (Wp.5 30M). If you're thinking of a lonely mountain top you're in for a surprise. Only twenty to fifty people are allowed on the summit in each two hour session, but this means that all of them are up here at once trying to bag a rock to sit on, or strolling around taking in the stupendous views of other Canary Islands, making for a crowded peak. You can never get enough of the views so it is with reluctance that we start the descent (0M).

N.B. We recommend pre-purchasing cable-car tickets online in advance at:

www.volcanoteide.com/en

- to avoid long queues and guarantee your time slot for the ascent.

Taking care on the steep trail as we drop down, we pass hikers labouring up the path, back to the ranger's control point (Wp.3 20M).

Bearing left, we're back amongst the tourists as we take the trail (*sendero* **Nº11**) out to the **Mirador de la Fortaleza** to cross a small *barranco* before reaching a small *mirador* platform (Wp.6 23M). Continuing on the well-walked rock trail we pass the **Montaña Blanca** trail junction (Wp.7 32M), but rather than immediately getting into our descent, we take the main trail out to the **Mirador de la Fortaleza** large viewing platform (Wp.8 33M) to take in the northern views; spectacular, but after the views from the peak only a consolation for those without a permit.

After the 'Peak' and 'Tourist' *miradors* it's time to set out (0M) on the big descent, so we backtrack to the **Montaña Blanca** trail (Wp.7), the National Park's official *sendero* **Nº7**, for the first stage of our descent to the **Refugio de Altavista**. After the well-made trails this is a rougher and pickier narrow path (E) requiring concentration on every step as we cross with the super-fit walkers on their ascent.

When the trail swings right into a switchback and the roof of the *refugio* is visible, a fainter path (look for a cairn on a big boulder) to the left off the main trail (Wp.9 17M) offers an interesting short detour to the **Ice Cave**. Less than

The refuge at Altavista

fifty metres away is the black maw of the **Cueva del Hielo** (Wp.10) where even in summer you are likely to find icicles. Sadly, the 5-metre vertical ladder down into the cave has been removed.

We pick our way down the main trail to emerge on the small plateau dominated by the substantial **Refugio de Altavista** (Wp.11 30M). There are comfortable rock walls to sit on so we take a break for a bit of lunch while enjoying the views across the crater to the opposite rim. The rooms open only in late afternoon for the hikers coming to overnight here, but the entrance hall opens at 11am; no real service, but at least there's vending machines with coffee and candy, and an internet wi-fi hotspot.

A Teide Egg (Wp.12)

Refreshed, we start out down the zigzagging trail (0M) from the refuge. We're winding down the face of the mountain before our trail runs out to an area of volcanic bombs (Wp.12 25M). If you can imagine a high misty, snow-capped, lonely mountain with a dragon roaring round its summit then its only a small leap of the imagination to see these bombs as 'dragons' eggs' though locally they are known as 'Huevos del Teide' (Teide eggs).

After photo opportunities we set off downward again to meet the **Montaña Blanca** track (Wp.13 47M). From this junction to the right, then left at a Y-junction 180 metres later, a broad stone-lined path goes to **Montaña Blanca** - an interesting detour for geologists, but offering little to no views from the flat summit plateau. Joe and myself decide to continue straight on down the track, the good surface giving us the luxury of striding out for the first time today, passing the 'trail shortcuts' across the *picón* slopes that cut off loops of the track; there are hefty fines for taking these shortcuts so stay on the main track! Passing a 'Teide Eggs' notice board (Wp.14 58M) we're bowling along at about 7km per hour when the orange flashes of runners pass us on their fast descent, soon to disappear into the distance. Following the winding track we pass a junction (Wp.15 68M) off to our left to **El Portillo** (official *senderos* **Nºs 6** and **22**), its lush oasis visible in the far distance, while our track turns south-east.

It's a bit of a monotonous finish as the track circles **Montaña Blanca** to pass the chained track of *sendero* **Nº27** (Wp.16 93M) and finally comes down past the vehicle barrier onto the TF-21 main (and only) road (Wp.17 105M). If you parked at the *teleférico* take new trail **Nº39** across the road bearing right (W). This in 3kms feeds into the **Sanatorio** track (**Nº16**) along which (NW) it's 1km to the cable-car station.

A short, interesting excursion into the maritime history of the **Anaga** provides for excellent views of **Igueste** and the coast as far as **Santa Cruz**, or even mighty **Teide**. At end of the trail we come to **El Semáforo** – a unique building in the Canaries which once played an important role in port operations of **Santa Cruz de Tenerife** sending maritime signals by using flags of different colours hoisted on a large mast, alerting arrivals of ships to the port. It was built by an English company in the late 19th century. The trail is well way-marked.

* Extension – extra 30 minutes
** **Bar Rincón de Anaga** at the very beginning of **Igueste** (closed Tuesdays)

Access by bus: bus Nº945 from **Santa Cruz** to the bus terminus in **Igueste**.

Access by car: Take the coastal TF-121 going NE from **Santa Cruz** to **Igueste de San Andrés**, where the road ends. Abundant parking is available anywhere along the road in **Igueste**, you can park just before the bus terminus (**Casas de Abajo**).

Wp.1, at the bus terminus

From the **Igueste** bus terminus (Wp.1 0M) we take the pedestrian railing-protected walkway (SSE), **Calle San Pedro**. Passing a church in **Plaza San Pedro** and a playground, we climb on broad stairs, **Caserío Casas de Abajo**, before bearing right in front of an orange house into a walkway past a water-tap and dragon tree.

Bearing left after descending down three steps we take the cemetery walkway, **Paseo Inciensal/Cementerio**, to a T-junction (Wp.2 9M), to the right is a descent to the beach, while we go left up stairs to another junction (Wp.3 10M) where we turn left onto a lava trail, while the branch ahead leads to the cemetery.

Our broad but rough trail is partially carved into the rock. We are soon rewarded by views back to **Igueste** and up to the **Anaga** ridge as we steadily ascend. Our climb brings us up to a viewpoint on a small rocky plateau/outcrop (Wp.4 26M).

The rocky outcrop, Wp.4

It is onwards and upwards for us to swing around a conical rock before finally coming to a Y-junction just below the ridge (Wp.5 48M).

El Semáforo (Wp.6)

Keeping straight ahead, our broad trail, intermittently protected by a low wall, soon drops and in a few minutes the remains of the 'mast' of **El Semáforo** come in sight. A steady downhill brings us to the old 'semaphore' building (Wp.6 60M) sitting within its fence.

From **Semáforo**, we retrace our outward route back to **Igueste**.

Extension: 30 mins return
If you fancy a small extension to ruins of a watchmen's cabin that preceded construction of **Semáforo** we take the path forking north from the Y-junction at Wp.5. It is generally narrower and rougher than the official trail, but never really exposed. The path climbs through groves of Canary spurge on the western slope, and soon joins a broader ridge. We bypass a rocky outcrop to its right before arriving at the ruins of **Casa de los Atalayeros** (**Atalaya de los Ingléses**) on the crest of the ridge, offering fine views.

Linking tip
From **Casa de los Atalayeros** (**Atalaya de los Ingléses**), an unofficial path continues north more or less following the ridge. The path circumvents a distinct dragon tree to its left, then traverses to the right above the tree, eventually connecting with our 'Igueste - Chamorga' route at Wp.7. At times the path is indistinct and overgrown making it only suitable for hikers with excellent path-finding skills.

An energetic hike, crossing the main **Anaga** ridge to link the two 'End-of-the-Road' villages of **Igueste de San Andrés** and **Chamorga**. From **Anaga**'s sun-drenched southern flanks into the lush-green forests of the central spine and beyond.

4 | 3¼ H | 9.4 km | 840m / 430m | one way | 2*

* **Bar Rincón de Anaga** in **Igueste** and **Bar Casa Alvaro** in **Chamorga**.

Access by bus: Nº945 from **Santa Cruz**. Get off at the bus stop just before the sharp-right bend of the road over a ravine in **Igueste**. There's an ATM at this bus stop. From **Chamorga**, Nº947 (only two afternoon departures a day).

Access by car: Take the coastal TF-11, then TF-121 going NE from **Santa Cruz** to **Igueste de San Andrés**, where the road ends. Street parking is available along the road in **Igueste**. This walk is a linear one-way route; however, car drivers could follow our route to the picturesquely-situated hamlet of **Lomo de las Casillas**, and then retrace our outward route back to **Igueste** (3H). If you have a car and want to do the whole route, you can park in **San Andrés** and from there take bus Nº945 to **Igueste**. The return bus Nº947 passes through **San Andrés** on its way to **Santa Cruz**.

Our itinerary follows the waymarked **PR TF 5** to **Chamorga**, whose mapboard and signpost are further down the road at the bus terminus in **Casas de Abajo**.

From the hairpin bend (Wp.1 0M), north of the ATM bus stop, we follow the **Carretera Lomo Bermejo** lane (N) into the ravine; also signed 'pista Hoya de los Juncos'. The lane runs along the watercourse, winding from one bank to the other, passing plots, houses and gardens before passing a right turn (Wp.2 15M) to a compound.

Starting at the bend (Wp.1)

After half an hour we pass a tiny concreted weir on our left and then, after a right-hand bend, bear right onto a sharply ascending concrete lane (Wp.3 31M) with a dead-end sign. After 100 metres we go left onto a waymarked stone trail, signed 'Las Casillas' (Wp.4 33M).

Our stone trail (Wp.4)

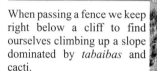

When passing a fence we keep right below a cliff to find ourselves climbing up a slope dominated by *tabaibas* and cacti.

At a small rocky plateau our trail swings east and continues on the top of a minor ridge, passing a roofed bench (Wp.5 51M). 50 metres on we pass an overgrown trail forking left to stay on the distinct, broad trail which then swings to the left side of the ridge before coming to a clump of trees protected behind a massive rock (Wp.6 57M). We then pass a rocky outcrop and another roofed bench before negotiating the final set of switchbacks to reach the main ridge line at a saddle (Wp.7 77M).

Lomo de las Casillas

Bearing left, we follow the wooden telephone poles (NW), our trail swinging over to the eastern, wooded side of the ridge before the houses of **Lomo de las Casillas** come into sight. Our trail leads us past a small shrine between the houses and 'La Beta Alan', fifty metres after which we bear left at a Y-junction (Wp.8 93M). Passing a pylon our path runs through a tunnel of trees to a second Y-junction (Wp.9 99M) where we go right on the descending path. Up and down shallow steps, in and out of the forest, we cross two streams, then pass a house built below a rock overhang (Wp.10 109M).

Our trail then climbs through stone steps, earth slopes and even a trench-like cutting, passing a small waterfall on our right, before finally emerging on the **Chamorga** road (Wp.11 118M). We go right on a wayposted lane (SE) and after 170 metres bear right at a Y-junction to pass the white walls of the cemetery, 25 metres after which, just before tarmac gives way to dirt, we bear left (N) onto a *camino* (Wp.12 123M), introduced by steps dropping into the forest. Tunnelling down the woodland path views open up across the valley to

Lomo de las Bodegas; with our onward route through the hamlet and on up to **La Cumbrilla** on top of the ridge. Our trail comes to a track where we go left (Wp.13 134M) to come past the first houses of **Lomo de las Bodegas**. At a Y-junction we bear right on a tarmac lane (Wp.14 140M), to immediately come to a parking area where we turn left onto a descending concrete walkway, then again left just before the steps dropping to the church. The walkway passes a patulous palm before it starts climbing steeply to **La Cumbrilla** on the ridge.

Passing vegetable plots we come to a Y-junction (Wp.15 149M) where we take the ascending left walkway. It then swings north-west to a driveway (Wp.16 151M) where we bear sharp right (E) to stay on the walkway and 30 metres later bear left on a steeply ascending walkway for our climb to reach the **La Cumbrilla** ridge (Wp.17 157M). Bearing left here (W), our way levels out to snake between houses, passing a *drago* tree and pylon, for us to come to a majestic conical rock at the end of the village.

At the foot of the rock, by a water tap, we bear right onto 'Camino La Cumbrilla' (Wp.18 160M). Our trail passes between abandoned houses before wading into the forest. After 3 minutes we bear left at a Y-junction (Wp.19 163M) after which it is a pleasant woodland stroll until we come to a junction to join the **PR TF 6** trail (Wp.20 180M).

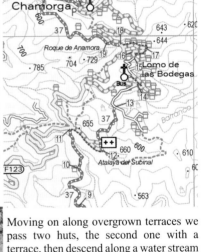

For those who fancy a scenic diversion via several *miradors* before finishing in **Chamorga**, bear left to climb for 700 metres to a forest crossroads of paths, to join our 'La Ensillada - Chamorga' route at its Wp.10. We however bear right, for a direct descent to **Chamorga**.

Finishing at Plaza Chamorga

Moving on along overgrown terraces we pass two huts, the second one with a terrace, then descend along a water stream choked with reeds. After a while we join a concrete walkway, ignoring stairs climbing steeply to our left, as we approach the village. Our trail becomes a cobbled walkway which finally emerges on a tarmac lane, just in front of **Plaza Chamorga** with a church (Wp.21 188M). Fifty metres to the right is a bus stop/terminus; to the left, it's 5 minutes to **Bar Casa Alvaro** for refreshments.

38

This adventure takes us through several climate zones and landscape types: Starting in **Cruz del Carmen**, often shrouded in clouds, we walk through a deep *laurisilva* forest, pass along eye-pleasing agriculture plots, to end up in a wild and sun-drenched landscape of jagged basalt crags. There's a natural swimming pool at **Punta del Hidalgo** offering a pleasant, safe dip.

(measured without **Mirador Aguaide** detour)

Access by bus: Most buses from **La Laguna** bus station into the **Anaga** pass through **Cruz del Carmen** giving a good choice for our outward ride (Nºs 76, 77, 273, 275). For our return the 50 and 105 run from **Punta del Hidalgo** to **La Laguna/Santa Cruz**.

Access by car: Not suitable for car drivers who could consider our Walk 39 'Cruz del Carmen Circular' adventure (actually a pan-handle).

Each side of **Bar/Rest Cruz del Carmen** are *sendero* boards; we choose the 'PR TF 10: Chinamada 5.3km, Punta del Hidalgo 9.7km' trail (Wp.1 0M). Immediately we're in the laurel forest on a broad woodland path which zigzags down with log-stepped sections (poor GPS reception in the forest).

As the trail levels out we pass a path off to our left (Wp.2 8M), our route curving round a large, steep wooded bowl in the *cumbre* to pass a second path (Wp.3).

Starting out at Wp.1, alongside the stone wall

After a short ascent we resume our inexorable descent through the trees. As we cross a ridge between two bowls (Wp.4 15M) a fainter walking trail goes straight ahead, while we go down a log-stepped descent into the second bowl. We catch glimpses of a dirt *pista* below us, before dropping onto the *pista* (Wp.5 19M) past a 'hitching rail' barring vehicle traffic.

Across the dirt track, a 'Carboneras, Chinamada, Taborno' sign points us down a steep trail, dropping down through tight zigzags into a sharp cleft and past a waterpoint, just before crossing the cleft's boggy watercourse (26M). We head steeply up in a slogging ascent, the gradient easing before we emerge from the forest onto a dirt track to the sight of brightly painted houses above us (Wp.6 28M).

Turning left, we head down the track past a cottage towards a *casita* and electricity pylon set on the next ridge. Ignoring tracks into the fields we keep heading downhill, our track narrowing to a trail (Wp.7). Ignoring a small path running ahead we start climbing steeply up and right to the electricity pylon and the tarmac road (Wp.8 42M).

Roque de Taborno seen from before Wp.10

Taking to the tarmac (NW), we pass a bus stop in the right bend and then, in the left bend, we leave the road at the three dragon trees (Wp.9 44M) on a trail to our right. We stroll along past colourful houses, soon on a narrow rural path to cross a dirt track while heading directly to the trees, before concrete steps take us down past a building onto the road (Wp.10 48M).

Crossing the road we follow the 'Chinamada, Carboneras' sign to go down manicured steps and head down the trail beneath a rock/earth cliff. Views open up over a ribbon of tarmac road way below us and across to **Roque de Taborno** in the distance. It's steeply down to a signed 'Chinamada, Carboneras' junction (Wp.11 52M) where we continue ahead on the **Chinamada** path towards the pylon; the right hand trail drops down to **Las Carboneras** (see Walk 39).

Contouring along beside a very steep ridge, we enjoy exceptional views before dropping down into the forest to a junction (Wp.12) where we keep right to climb back to our contouring altitude. We reach a goat farm *casita* sited above caves cut in the golden volcanic rock (Wp.13 67M), an idyllic picnic setting if you're taking a break.

From the *casita* our path contours round a steep wooded bowl before dropping to pass long-abandoned terraces, then we climb to excellent views on a corner (Wp.14 74M). Again, our route contours across the steep slopes, passing abandoned terraces before topping a crest (Wp.15) (just a few steps to the left off the main trail is another great viewpoint) to find sections of the original boulder-laid *camino real*. Our route crosses to the eastern side of the ridge, a minor path at a small shrine going off to our right (Wp.16 87M), where there's the opportunity to shortcut if you're doing Walk 39.

Chinamada in sight ahead

We go straight on, **Chinamada** coming into sight as we descend steadily to a *mirador* viewpoint. Dropping from the *mirador*, our path runs down past a cave with carved seat, to come onto a driveway at the first house and onto the road from **Las Carboneras** (Wp.17 96M) below a small red house.

Bearing left on the road, we stroll down below more cave houses built into a promontory to a parking area adjacent to the gaudily painted village square; on our right **Bar La Cueva** is built into the rock (closed Mon & Tues). For a short diversion starting from behind the plaza (Wp.18 101M) we recommend following the 'Mirador Aguaide' sign to overlook the massive rock eruption out of the *barranco* floor; approx 8 minutes each way.

Walk 39 now leaves us to take the road to Las Carboneras.

30 metres south-west of the **Chinamada** plaza, we take the broad paved trail ('Punta del Hidalgo 90 min.') to descend on elegant stairs (W) before passing cultivated fields and terraced vines. Soon we leave the cultivation behind to find ourselves in a landscape of eroded basalt crags.

We pass a small *mirador* secured by a railing, and meet a faint path from **Mirador Aguaide** which joins us from the right (Wp.19 113M). Steadily descending on rough bedrock, we have views into the *barranco* as we come to a small *mirador* (Wp.20 121M), from where we have a view of a bizarre rocky bridge, situated on the top of the ridge right in front of us.

Moving on, we negotiate a broad carved stairway under a rock overhang (see photo on next page), and just after a right bend, we find ourselves in front an exposed red-orange colourful rock face (Wp.21 128M).

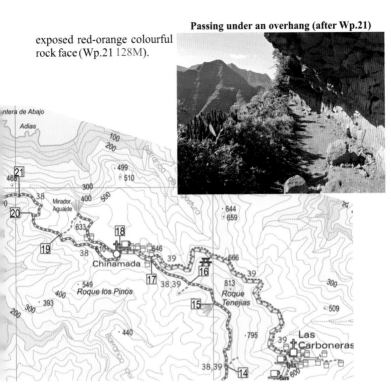

Passing under an overhang (after Wp.21)

For the adventurous, an almost invisible turn-off to the right, starting with a traverse of a rocky ledge, leads to the bizarre rocky bridge that tops the ridge above us (10 minutes one way, only for absolutely surefooted walkers, who don't mind potentially getting scratched by cacti and some light scrambling).

We continue our descent to pass another impressive overhang and then a series of carved steps, before coming to a railed *mirador* viewpoint (Wp.22 141M), backed by a huge black-red rock and a natural bench.

Our trail continues along the railing, then swings left (SW) in front of the double-headed **Roque Dos Hermanos** to descend in tight, yet comfortable switchbacks. After passing a series of caves (Wp.23 163M), our trail runs through a gully and soon joins a large dry stone wall, just before climbing down the broad paved stairs into the bed of the *barranco* (Wp.24 186M).

We either turn right to follow the streambed for a short detour to **Playa de los Troches** beach (Wp.25 189M), or directly cross over it to climb out on a track around two industrial buildings onto the driveway of a house. Continuing straight on we pass a barrier to walk beside a banana plantation, before coming to a T-junction (Wp.26 199M), where we bear left.

Just a few metres up the lane we reach a small circular plaza with a bus terminus (Wp.27 201M), from where we can catch a bus back. Or, if there's time, continue along the road for 800 metres, where we find bars and a pastry shop opposite a church and another bus-stop (Wp.28 211M). The sea-water pool is a further 1km down the road.

39

We're following the first half of Walk 38 to produce a pan-handle circular route, taking in **Las Carboneras** (with its refreshment options) before our ascent back to **Cruz del Carmen**. An excellent forest and ridges route, even if it does have some tarmac to link **Chinamada** to **Las Carboneras**.

Access by bus: Same as Walk 38. From **Las Carboneras** bus Nº275, should you decide to finish your hike here.

Access by car: Park on the extensive parking area by the *ermita* at **Cruz del Carmen**.

Wp.17, meeting Las Carboneras road

Our outward route is the same as Walk 38 (Wps.1 to 18, 0-101M). There's the option to turn right at Wp.16 (shrine) or Wp.17 (tarmac lane), though the stroll to **Chinamada** (refreshments) and the short extension to **Mirador Aguaide** (great views) are well worth completing the full route.

From **Chinamada** (Wp.18 101M), we follow the tarmac lane to **Las Carboneras** - an easy stroll downhill but we have rather a relentless slog uphill on the tarmac which might make the opportunity of a lane-side picnic area (Wp.19 113M) too good to miss. The lane brings us to a stairway with handrail on our right (Wp.20 119M): a path climbs away steeply at first, then traverses the slope high above the lane to rejoin it 750 metres later (Wp.21). The path offers spectacular views over **Barranco de Taborno** and across to **Roque de Taborno**, but as it is mildly vertiginous, vertigo sufferers better stay on the lane. The final steeper section of the lane takes us into **Las Carboneras**, panting gratefully up to the doors of **Bar/Rest Tesegre** (Wp.22 138M), just below the village square and bus stop.

The final stage in our adventure is mostly uphill, as we set off from the bus stop (0M) to stroll down past **Bar/Rest Valentin** opposite the signed trail for 'Taborno' (Wp.23) and leave the settlement behind. 150 metres after passing a sports ground, we find the stairway (Wp.24 6M) climbing up from the road for a steep, staired ascent until the gradient eases to merely steep.

We slog up through bracken and tree heather, our ascent relenting as we round the spur and the pylon comes into sight. A *fuente* provides a welcome break in the ascent (Wp.25 22M 727m), shortly before we climb back up to the path junction at Wp.11 (see photo on the next page).

You'll well remember the outward route in reverse; a steep ascent to cross the

Wp.11, start of the circular leg

road, a short tarmac stroll from the three *dragos* before turning off on our outward path, easy up to the outlying *casita* then slog up to the houses and dive back into the forest, zig-zagging up to the *pista* then past the 'hitching rail' to climb up through the forest in a stiff ascent, emerging alongside the bar at **Cruz del Carmen** (83M). The laurel forest saves us from the sun but it's still a gruelling three hundred metre ascent in any language, the bar's ice cold Dorada tasting like nectar - but what wouldn't we pay for a bar stool to perch on!

40

The road along the **Anaga**'s spine makes a good jumping-off point for adventures in this dramatic landscape. Modern tarmac roads to **Taborno** and **Las Carboneras** are dramatic enough, but the old *camino real* trails of the donkey power days are far more breathtaking, particularly on the uphill return. This is one of those spinal routes, dramatic in descent as well as ascent; with the option to bus back from **Taborno**. Car drivers should consider parking at **Taborno** then ascending to **Casa Carlos** for refreshments before returning.

| 3 | 2H | 5 km | 350m / 350m | out & back * | 3 ** |

Casa Carlos (Wp.1)

* or one-way downhill trip to **Taborno**, with the bus back. Can be also combined with Walk 41

** at **Casa Carlos** (closed Tuesdays) and in **Taborno** at **Restaurante Historias Para No Dormir** (closed Mon-Wed)

Access by bus:
From **La Laguna** bus Nº76 links **La Laguna** to **Afur**, Nº77 to **El Bailadero**. Alight at **Casa Carlos**, a well known road-side restaurant. You need to ask the bus driver to drop you off at **Casa Carlos**, the actual bus stop for the eastbound buses being 60 metres before reaching the restaurant, 50 metres past **Las Carboneras/Taborno** road junction. You can also use bus Nº275 and get off at the **Las Carboneras/Taborno** junction, 110 metres west of the start. For a descent-only option, you have the 275 from **Taborno** to **La Laguna**.

Access by car: some parking places at (and behind) **Casa Carlos** restaurant on the TF-12 (make sure to have at least a drink to justify your stay). There are some on-road car spaces before entering **Taborno** but take care not to block the bus-turning circle.

We go down the lane (NE) beside

Casa Carlos (Wp.1 0M) signed 'Taborno'. The tarmac becomes concrete, then strips by house N°64, before narrowing to a trail and plunging into the forest. Straight down a narrow spur (N), whose sheer sides could be considered forested cliffs we keep straight on at a staggered crossroads with a path (Wp.2 5M) before passing house N°66 set beside the trail (Wp.3 7M).

After picking our way down the trail, we are greeted by a drawbridge-like dirt path a metre wide, across the flat top of a very steep-sided natural earth bank that links us to the next rocky promontory; it's so neat, you'd think it was man-made. After a second dirt 'drawbridge' our trail reverts to its original nature as laurel is replaced by tree heather and eucalyptus alongside the route before passing an earth cave with seat (Wp.4 16M).

The **Taborno** road is a narrow ribbon far below as we head relentlessly down the ridge, zigzagging through tree heather to a natural *mirador* (Wp.5 22M) with spectacular views over the **Barranco de Afur**. We cross another 'drawbridge' for an unusual slight upward incline, followed by a rock-stair ascent to the **Afur** junction (Wp.6 26M) where the descent to the settlement drops steeply down to our right to meet our Walk 41 in 400 metres.

The shrine at Wp.7

Turning left, our broad dirt trail curves around the mountainside above steep drops to the little road way below to pass a small shrine (Wp.7 31M) set in the rock before descending again, now with ridge-top views. A slight

Views before Wp.8

ascent to a fenced water tank (Wp.8 38M), then a steep, sometimes stepped, descent towards **Taborno** before a final concrete slope bringing us down to the road at the entrance to the village (Wp.9 46M) and its bus terminus.

Approaching Taborno (Wp.9)

Houses cling to the narrow ridge as we skitter down the steep street past the restaurant before we bottom out at the square in front of a chapel (Wp.10 50M 638m), a comfortable spot from which to take in the extensive views to east and west.

41

This tour has everything we could wish for! Spectacular landscapes, primeval forests, ridge-top views, a ravine known as 'small Masca' and a beach. It passes through several villages, meaning that refreshments are evenly distributed along our way. We finish in **Taganana**, a region renowned for its wine making. In the last third views to the spectacular **Roque de las Ánimas** and **Roque en Medio** open up to offer a grand finale; these pointy formations towering high up to the sky are sure to catch your eye until the very end in **Taganana**. The walk can be combined or split in various ways: it can be started in **Taborno**, started or finished in **Afur** (bus connections in both villages), or split into two parts.

5* 4½ H 14.3 km 750m / 1200m one way ** 4

* the route can be tailored to shorter variants
** vertiginous sections are between **Afur** and **Playa de Tamadiste** and are in most cases protected by railing

Access by bus: Nº275 from **La Laguna** goes to **Las Carboneras/Taborno**. Depending on the schedule, it goes first to **Taborno** before calling in **Las Carboneras** and vice-versa. Bus Nº76 serves **Afur** from **La Laguna** and the 946 connects **Taganana** with **Santa Cruz**.

Access by car: This route is not suitable for car drivers. See our Walk 42 'Taganana Circular' for a car based route.

Our lane drops down at Wp.2

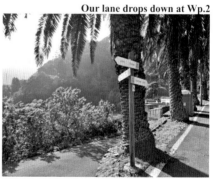

From the bus terminus in **Las Carboneras** (Wp.1 0M) we stroll back down the road to take the narrow tarmac lane signed 'Taborno', opposite **Bar/Rest Valentin** (Wp.2 2M), where there's a bus stop. Our lane drops down into the valley, swinging left after 60 metres where a wooden 'Taborno' sign directs us down onto a small path.

We drop down onto the narrow walking trail running between the lane's support wall and vegetable plots before a rock stepped descent, needing careful footwork, takes us down past more plots in a side valley of the main *barranco*. Vegetation pushes in on our path (secateurs useful) which then surprisingly climbs gently up past white rock, widening to a comfortable walking width as it cuts across the steep wooded slopes before passing an electricity pylon (Wp.3 8M).

Passing a small *teleférico*, its wire stretching up to the edge of the road high above us, we curve around the *barranco* wall to another electricity pylon (Wp.4) marking our transit into another pocket in its wall. A picky descent on rock steps takes us around a ruined hut camouflaged by vegetation, before

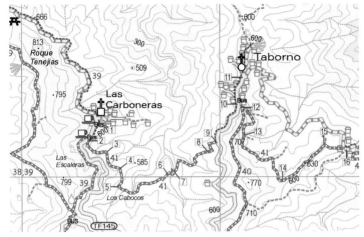

continuing down through zigzags, vigorous plant-life enveloping the path - careful footwork needed. We come to a potato and pumpkin patch and pass below a green hut (Wp.5 16M). There's only one path across the *barranco* and as this is the last vegetable plot, our route is likely to be less walked and consequently more overgrown from this point. Another rock zigzag descent takes us across a watercourse, then our path pushes through a briar and bracken section before we enter into a section of tree heather.

Our path winds amongst the steep forested slopes with just one more briar and bracken section before emerging into the open (Wp.6 25M) to see **Taborno** above us across the ravine. A steady to steep descent drops us down to follow a watercourse which our path then crosses (Wp.7). It's an easy guess that we're in for some serious climbing as our path heads steeply up the slope. After an energetic climb we finally come into the open to traverse a plot along a high stone wall (Wp.8 38M). We climb up to an electricity pylon, just above which, at a turn in the path, is a tiny shrine to 'Señora Dona Effizez Carlos (1934)' set in a stone wall. A final slogging ascent brings us up to emerge gratefully onto the **Taborno** road (Wp.9 43M), where we swing left. After that tough climb the gently sloping tarmac feels like luxury as we reach the bus terminus at the beginning of **Taborno** village (Wp.10 50M); our Walk 40 ridge line route from **Casa Carlos** also joins the road at this point. A simple stroll down the main street takes us to the luxury of wooden benches on the village square below the chapel (Wp.11 54M).

Taborno to Afur
Back at Wp.10, we climb onto a skewed wall, with a signpost (Wp.12 59M). Heading east we take the concrete trail resembling a covered water-canal and ignore a concrete *camino* dropping to our left as we traverse the valley. Maintaining height, we go above terraces, through blackberry shrubs and ferns before coming to a Y-junction (Wp.13 66M). We go right here followed by turning right at another junction a few minutes later to climb rock steps and pass a tiny cave with a bench. Passing through an improvised palette gate, we negotiate steps to emerge on a ridge top (Wp.14 77M) at a signpost, stunning views into the valley opening in front of us.

Turning left (NE), we follow the ridge, forest line on our left. When views

Towards the 'chicken-coop house' (Wp.16)

open up on our left, we bear right (Wp.15 85M) (a faint goat trail continues ahead) to begin our steep descent towards the hamlet of **El Frontón**, in sight below us. Going down the concrete steps above a white house we cross its tarmac driveway (Wp.16 91M) to take a trail for **Afur** signed with a 'wooden finger'. Our trail swings right in front of an orange house (rather resembling a giant chicken coop) to descend across a cactus covered slope. We pass a white house (Nº16) and several vegetable plots before our trail swings left (E). It is soon joined by a path from the right (Wp.17 107M) before joining a concreted *camino* as we approach the

houses of **Lomo Centeno** hamlet. Our trail brushes by a gravel parking area (Wp.18 115M) from where we have our first views of **Barranco de Afur**.

Descending on a lamppost-lined *camino*, we reach the bottom of the ravine, where we cross a bridge over the brook before bearing left at a junction (Wp.19 124M). Crossing a second bridge a brief climb takes us into **Afur**. At a T-junction with a cobbled lane, we

head left ('PR TF 8 Taganana 7.5km') to the small plaza (Wp.20 129M), while to our right is a bus stop.

Afur to Taganana
From the plaza we pass **Bar/Rest Cantina**, then a school, before bearing right at a T-junction after the last houses (Wp.21 132M), taking a descending dirt path lined by

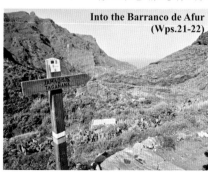

Into the Barranco de Afur (Wps.21-22)

cacti and aloe. Crossing a concrete lane and a parallel dirt track, we enter the silent **Barranco de Afur**. The beautiful trail runs along a rugged basalt face with a streambed in the sheer depths below us.

The impressive cleft (Wps.23-24)

Turning sharp right at a Y-junction (Wp.22 140M) we cross over a crest, then negotiate stretches intermittently protected by a railing to cross another crest (Wp.23 147M). Descending on steep steps followed by tight switchbacks we come down to the water.

Crossing the stream we zigzag between the reeds before climbing out of the ravine on a narrow rock-carved *camino* with handrail to pass an impressive broad cleft before reaching a crest top with views to both sides (Wp.24 150M).

From the crest our trail drops gently and crosses two gullies to climb briefly before reaching a ridge (Wp.25 158M) with a small plateau for our first glimpse of **Playa de Tamadiste**. We descend towards terraces set on the steep slopes before we cross them. Our trail drops further down towards the streambed before it briefly climbs and runs through a cleft in a natural wall marked with a waymark (Wp.26 171M). A vertiginous path from **Taborno** feeds in from our left here. Depending on the season there is a waterfall running through the mouth of the wall, creating a pool deep enough for a refreshing dip.

We walk near the *barranco* floor on its left side and spot a trail to **Taganana** climbing to the right from the streambed (Wp.27 175M). First, we continue on to the beach, either climbing up to the left over a rock to pass a beach house, or simply following the streambed winding though the reeds to reach **Playa de Tamadiste** (Wp.28 177M).

After a break we follow the stream back to Wp.27 and take the **Taganana** trail (E). It climbs steadily passing a shack and neglected terraces, before the gradient moderates.

We get our first views of **Roques de Anaga** projecting from the ocean far in the distance before reaching a small saddle (Wp.29 198M), from where we can see the spectacular **Roque de las Ánimas** and **Roque en Medio**.

The spectacular Roques

These pointy rocks serve well for our navigation as they sit just above **Taganana** and we soon catch our first view of the village. Across several gullies, the last one really deep-cut above a sheer gorge, we emerge at the end of a dirt track at a welcoming picnic place (Wp.30 228M).

We follow the track, dirt with some concrete, passing several notice boards on winemaking and after 10 minutes from the first board we bear right along a water pipe, following a waymarked path climbing away from the track (Wp.31 248M). We join a tarmac lane, which we follow for 50 metres to a white house on the corner (Wp.32 255M).

Our concrete trail, **Calle Lomo La Chanca**, drops steeply left into the village in switchbacks before crossing a tarmac lane to come to a T-junction (Wp.33 261M). Here we take the lane to the right. A narrow street takes us to another T-junction, where we bear right, passing a small plaza before crossing a bridge. The cobbled street passes **Taganana**'s main fountain in sight of the church (Wp.34 267M). Trees at the plaza provide welcome shade, while a bar and a supermarket are on the other side of the plaza. We bear right before the church, then left and right to pass **Bar/Rest Casa Picar** on the corner. The tarmac lane then takes us down onto the main road to a bus stop (Wp.35 270M).

Car drivers do not have to miss out on the delights of the **Barranco de Afur** and the imposing *roques*, as our circular route out of **Taganana** combines much of Walk 41's adventures with a finish back where we started.

Access by bus: Nº946 from **Santa Cruz**.

Our start at the bus stop (Wp.1)

Access by car: park your car in a lay-by next to dumpsters and a bus stop, just where a lane (**Calle Los Artesanos**) to the left rises from the main road (from the main road you'll see the green billboard of **Bar Casa Picar** high up the lane).

Wp.2, Taganana Church

From the bus stop on the main road south-east of **Taganana** (Wp.1 0M) we take the **Calle Los Artesanos** lane that climbs left and parallels the main road to **Bar/Rest Casa Picar**, where we swing left around the corner and immediately right onto **Calle Canonigo Juan Negrin**. This takes us to a T-junction beside the church (Wp.2 3M) by a pleasant shady plaza.

Bearing left, we pass the main fountain of **Taganana** to cross a cobbled bridge after which we bear right, past a pharmacy and a small plaza. We go up **Caserío San Antonio** and, when the tarmac gives way to cobbles, go left into the narrow **Calle Lomo La Chanca** (Wp.3 6M).

Bearing left at a T-junction (Wp.4) and crossing a tarmac lane we climb on the urban trail to emerge facing a white house with green door (Wp.5 16M) where we meet our return route.

Turning left, we continue on a concrete lane lined with white houses. At the end of the houses we swing right on an ascending concrete driveway passing **Casa Noni**, immediately after which we go left on a level dirt track that beautifully contours the whole valley; the **La Cumbrecilla** pass with its pylon visible ahead of us.

10 minutes later, following a concreted section which turns into a cobbled track, we bear left at a Y-junction of cobbled tracks/driveways and then, in front of terraces, we go right up broad stone steps onto the *camino* signed 'La Cumbrecilla' (Wp.6 33M).

Roughly following an electricity line we pass a cottage, then a grove of reeds and a solitary house before wading into the shade of the forest. Our relentless ascent on the trail brings us up to the **La Cumbrecilla** pass (Wp.7 60M), the views rewarding our exertion.

Climbing to La Cumbrecilla (Wps.6-7)

Our trail from La Cumbrecilla (Wp.7)

From the pass, we take the **Afur** trail (NNW) to plunge back into the forest below a jagged rocky ridge.

A gently descending trail takes us out of the forest, across abandoned terraces, to come down to a *finca* (Wp.8 74M) from which we descend on a concrete lane.

5 minutes later at a Y-junction we bear right to drop down to a second homestead, where we swing right between the houses (Wp.9 81M) onto a rather discreet path lined with tall vegetation.

After descending a slope rich with aloe and cacti, we bear left at a T-junction (Wp.10 85M), soon going through a grove of reeds to emerge on the **Afur** road (Wp.11 88M).

Turning right we stroll down the road. 180 metres after the Km6 marker, we bear left onto a concrete trail protected by a railing (Wp.12 101M). Our trail runs under an impressive rock overhang and soon comes to a T-junction with a cobbled lane next to a dragon tree (Wp.13 107M) in **Afur** where we bear left down to a small community plaza (108M - Wp.20 of Walk 41).

From the plaza, we follow the descriptions and waypoints from Walk 41. Note that on the map and in the waypoint file, Wps.21 to 31 of Walk 41 are renumbered to Wps.14 to 24 of Walk 42.

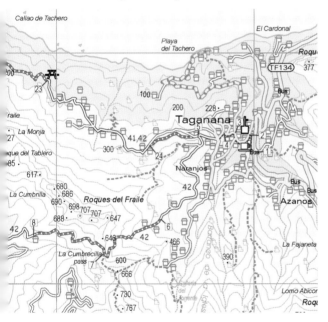

43

A ridge-top route with plenty of surprises and a delightful descent into the 'end-of-the-road' village of **Chamorga**. Spectacular *miradors* combine with woodland and spectacular flora to produce a true classic in every sense of the word. Paths are generally narrow requiring sure-footedness but are not vertiginous, at least in our experience.

Permit restrictions: A free access permit is necessary for the section of this route between **La Ensillada** (Wp.1) and **Cabezo del Tejo** (Wp.9). This is due to conservation of **El Pijaral**, one of the finest examples of misty forest on the Canary Islands, with high scientific and botanical value.

To obtain a permit go to: centralreservas.tenerife.es (Spanish only at the time of writing) where a list of activities is shown. Select 'Recorrido a pie por el sendero de El Pijaral', select a date from the calendar and fill out your name and ID/Passport number. You'll receive your confirmation number and details which you can either save or send to your email. Print out a copy or load it onto your smart phone/device for presentation. A maximum of 45 visitors per day are allowed. The booking can be made 3 months ahead and the limit of people in a group is 5 per booking (for more than 5 make two or more bookings). Only private visitors (non-profit groups) are permitted.

4   2¼H   7.5 km   300m / 600m   one way   1

Access by bus: This linear route takes advantage of the Nº947 Titsa bus to **Chamorga**; only two pm departures, so time your arrival accordingly.

Access by car: Park in the **La Ensillada** car park on the north side of the TF-123, 4.8km from **El Bailadero**.

Starting from the parking area (Wp.1 0M) we follow a dirt track into the forest (NE) parallel to the road. Immediately we plunge into the dank forest (poor GPS reception). We stroll uphill, our track narrowing to a trail (Wp.2), becoming stone-stepped on the steeper sections.

Ancient trees and lichen give the forest a fairy tale air as we curve up (N) to a junction (Wp.3 14M).

Going left on the minor path, we continue ascending (W) through the trees, glimpses of vast drops through the tall

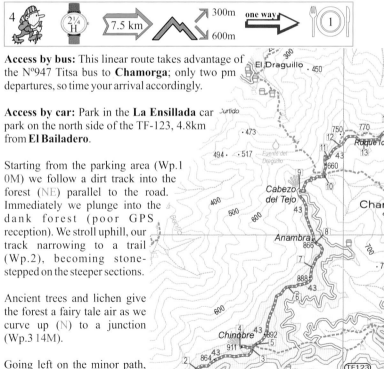

heather on our right revealing that we're climbing along the edge of cliffs.

A final climb and clamber on rock bring us onto the summit of **Chinobre** (Wp.4 17M 924m); a broad rocky knob with trig point, poking above the trees like a geological periscope. On a good day the views can unman even the most resolute poet. We return to the main path (Wp.3 0M) to continue towards **Cabezo del Tejo**.

We have an easy stroll down through the forest on the well-defined path, earth/mud stepped sections requiring careful footwork, to a trail junction (Wp.5 2M). Our route continues ahead as a pleasant woodland path running alongside the eastern edge of a ridge, generally downhill with steeper earth/mud stepped sections, but climbing a small crest before passing an impressive rock perched on the lip of the ridge (Wp.6 11M).

It's pleasant strolling until a stepped ascent takes us to another crest, then our woodland path crosses to the western side of the ridge (Wp.7) with impressive views and drops, glimpsed through the trees on our left. We're brought up short on this pleasant descent of the wooded ridge as we emerge from the trees to come nose to nose with the great rock of **Anambra** (Wp.8 24M) - a greater contrast between woodland and this sheer pinnacle of rock soaring skyward would be difficult to find.

When we've had our fill of looking, we follow the path around **Anambra** to plunge down into the forest once more.

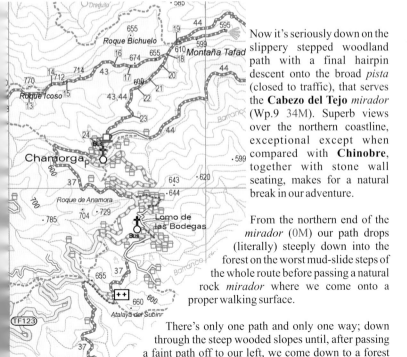

Now it's seriously down on the slippery stepped woodland path with a final hairpin descent onto the broad *pista* (closed to traffic), that serves the **Cabezo del Tejo** *mirador* (Wp.9 34M). Superb views over the northern coastline, exceptional except when compared with **Chinobre**, together with stone wall seating, makes for a natural break in our adventure.

From the northern end of the *mirador* (0M) our path drops (literally) steeply down into the forest on the worst mud-slide steps of the whole route before passing a natural rock *mirador* where we come onto a proper walking surface.

There's only one path and only one way; down through the steep wooded slopes until, after passing a faint path off to our left, we come down to a forest crossroads of paths on a saddle, (Wp.10 9M). A 25 minute shortcut to **Chamorga** drops steeply to our right, the hamlet of **El Draguillo** is down to our left. Carrying straight on across the crossroads, we climb steadily and then steeply on the woodland path to pass a natural rock *mirador* (Wp.11 13M), then a more vertiginous dirt *mirador* before finally slogging up to a crest (Wp.12 17M).

At the *mirador* near Wp.15

Over the crest, the narrow woodland path circles a bowl. We pass below spurs of rock (Wp.13) before arriving at a spectacular *mirador* (Wp.14 27M) set at the top of cliffs overlooking the **Roques de Anaga**; we'd advise you not to put any trust in the wooden railings. After the *mirador* we get glimpses of **Chamorga** as

we head steeply uphill through stunted forest to a path junction (Wp.15 31M) to yet another *mirador* (20-metres detour along the left branch), followed by a rock outcrop (Wp.16 40M), making a break from the woodland.

Views of Roques de Anaga from Wp.14

Finally we leave the woods behind (Wp.17) to walk across heather-covered slopes with

The *drago* just visible on Tafada ridge

views over the **Barranco de Roque Bermejo**. Endemic flora competes for star billing alongside our path as we come down to a junction (Wp.18), our final route to **Chamorga** going back right, but we carry straight on before coming down onto the saddle at another path junction by the **Tafada** ruined cottage (Wp.19 50M).

From the saddle we have options to go on past the **Tafada** cottage to overlook the **Faro de Anaga** (ENE); simply follow the ridge line past the solitary *drago*. The views open up 100 metres after the tree. Or you could descend past the *faro* on Walk 44 to **Roque Bermejo**, and then return to **Chamorga** on the path up the **Barranco de Roque Bermejo**; in this case bear left after 100 metres from the ruined cottage to take the waymarked path (NE).

After enjoying these beautiful surroundings, we backtrack to the junction

(Wp.18 0M) to take the **Chamorga** path (SW), one of the **Anaga**'s most delightful paths though requiring surefootedness on its narrow sections and clambering descents, initially onto a well trodden path (Wp.20), where the actual descent begins.

We angle down towards **Chamorga** across the flora-stuffed slopes to a set of handrails (Wp.21 6M) above a 'rock-stair' descent before the easy path resumes.

On the descent at Wp.21

Our next feature is a geologically interesting rock-stepped descent alongside a sloping cliff face, to come onto the luxury of a metre-wide comfortable dirt path taking us past the first terraces (Wp.22 10M) before coming up onto a spur (Wp.23 15M) below a massive 'Devil's Head' rock while the spur is tipped by an oversize 'Friar's Rock'.

Our final descent is straightforward, to come down and curve above the first houses of the settlement before dropping down to the tarmac road (Wp.24 24M) right in front of **Bar Casa Alvaro**. Following the street to the right we come past the church to the bus terminus (28M). Do tell the driver that you want to get off at **La Ensillada** when boarding and paying, if you have your car there.

44

Chamorga really is the 'end of the line'. Its bus terminus is also the end of the tarmac road, but at least it has a basic bar. Scanning the sharp ridges that surround the village and its steep *barranco* running down to the sea, you know that any circular walking route based on the village is going to be well up the 'exertion' rating. Our medium level great adventure climbs to the saddle then strides along the **Anaga**'s airiest ridge to a spectacular viewing point, before descending on the traditional **Faro de Anaga** trail to the almost abandoned **Roque Bermejo** hamlet, with an option to descend a bit further down to the beach. All those descents have to be paid for on the final section as we ascend the spectacular *barranco* on an immaculate trail; the bar's a good incentive for tired legs during the long, seemingly endless, ascent! If you're fit enough yet only have time for one **Anaga** route, this should be your first choice. In May, white *tajinastes* are common on the north-eastern flanks of **Montaña Tafada**, look for them around the trail on your way down to the *faro*.

| 4 | 2¾ H | 8 km | 680m / 680m | ↻ | 1 |

Access by car:
From **El Bailadero** follow the twisty TF-123. When it finally drops steeply off the ridge, park before the start of **Chamorga** village by the bus

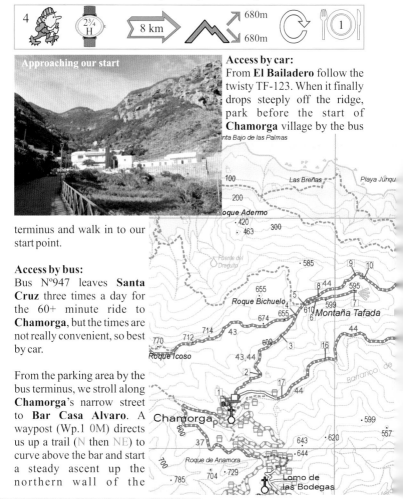

terminus and walk in to our start point.

Access by bus:
Bus Nº947 leaves **Santa Cruz** three times a day for the 60+ minute ride to **Chamorga**, but the times are not really convenient, so best by car.

From the parking area by the bus terminus, we stroll along **Chamorga**'s narrow street to **Bar Casa Alvaro**. A waypost (Wp.1 0M) directs us up a trail (N then NE) to curve above the bar and start a steady ascent up the northern wall of the *barranco* towards a 'Devil's Head' rock, Walk 43 in reverse. The views become even more impressive as we ascend and endemic flora crowds the steep slopes either side of our well-maintained trail as we reach the devil's head (Wp.2 10M). Our trail turns into and contours round a floriferous side valley before climbing again. As our climb tops out at the head of the final stair (Wp.3 19M) it's back to easy walking as our narrow trail winds over the ridge (NE) to overlook the ruin of **Casa Tafada** on the saddle below us. A bit of a picky descent, not helped by abundant flora hiding small drops in the path, takes us down to the ridge line (Wp.4 23M) shortly before we step onto the saddle (Wp.5 24M) next to ruined cottages.

From the cottages (0M), we stick to the official trail climbing along the ridge (ENE), to a path junction (Wp.6 2M) where we keep straight on, to take a short diversion on **Montaña Tafada** and head towards the *drago* tree and further on to the end of the promontory. Views elsewhere on our route are impressive but from the end of the airy **Tafada** ridge (Wp.7 10M) they are nothing less than spectacular and include the vista down over our route including the lighthouse. We pick our way back along the rocky trail to the junction (Wp.6).

Taking the official trail down off the ridge (Wp.6 0M) we have a steep, and slippery when wet, descent through broom and tree heather to a junction where the trail from the ruins joins us from the left (Wp.8 2M). Turning right (E), directions are superfluous as we follow the well-walked trail gently down across slopes simply packed with endemic flora. The dramatic islands of **Roques de Anaga** come into view as we come down onto a rock sheet (Wp.9 9M) where small cairns guide us to our trail's continuation.

We curve round below the bulk of **Tafada** and the *faro* comes into view, closer now but still a long way below us. After a natural rock seat (Wp.10 11M) our trail makes a serious rock descent with stepped and zigzag sections before running out across alpine meadow style slopes to take the line of a ridge running down from **Tafada**. In places the trail has a skittery surface making for slow progress relieved by views down into **Barranco de Roque Bermejo** as we head for the lighthouse's cupola; and what views they are - just look at those

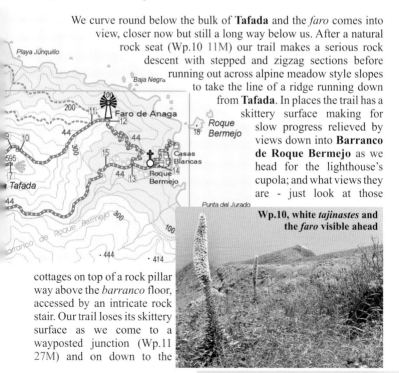

Wp.10, white *tajinastes* and the *faro* visible ahead

cottages on top of a rock pillar way above the *barranco* floor, accessed by an intricate rock stair. Our trail loses its skittery surface as we come to a wayposted junction (Wp.11 27M) and on down to the fenced **Faro de Anaga** (Wp.12 29M), less impressive close to. From the *faro* a substantial dirt road winds down into the valley, a rather tiresome trudging descent zigzagging across steep barren slopes alleviated slightly by a short paved section before we reach the valley floor and a signed junction (Wp.13 45M). 'Chamorga' is signed right while we follow the 'Roque Bermejo' sign down past plots to the almost abandoned hamlet and its *ermita* (Wp.14 49M). **Roque Bermejo** might be Tenerife's most isolated community; we saw nobody but walkers and a hungry ginger cat. The *ermita* could do with some TLC but the messages inside to a recent walking accident death are a sage reminder not to be casual in our approach to these landscapes.

Playa de Roque Bermejo

You can continue down to **Playa Roque Bermejo**, either on the path across the valley floor or on the stepped descent from the *ermita*; after all you'll probably only be here once, so make the most of it. The tiny 'bar' - actually just a lady selling beer and soda from her house - next to the beach is open usually just on weekends, provided the sea is calm enough to bring in the supplies.

Postponing the final climb to Chamorga (Wps.15-16)

You can guess our final stage - yes, a slogging ascent up the *barranco* back to **Chamorga** (0M). It's quite a pull back up to the junction (Wp.13), then the steady ascent continues relentlessly. Remember that intricate stair we saw from the ridge line? It's instant recall as we start up its stepped ascent (Wp.15 10M), admiring views from the ruined cottages at the stair top after which we're back on more reasonable gradients. **Barranco de Roque Bermejo** is a beautiful ravine, the trail well maintained as it twists and turns away from the ravine. It's onwards and upwards, alleviated by a few gentler sections and rests until finally a building comes into view (Wp.16 46M).

Past a hut and up the trail we pass the first house (Wp.17 57M) with the heartening view of the village ahead. Our trail widens into a dirt road (the signed trail leaves the road only to rejoin it a few minutes later) which we follow up to the edge of the village (70M) where we intend to heartily support the modest local hostelry, **Bar Casa Alvaro**.

This glossary contains Spanish and Canarian words found in the text (shown in *italics*) plus other local words that you may encounter.

abandonado	abandoned, in poor repair	*cordillera*	mountain range
		correos	post office
abierto	open	*cortijo*	farmstead
acequia	water channel	*costa*	coast
aeropuerto	airport	*coto privado*	private hunting
agua	water	*de caza*	area
agua no potable	water (not drinkable)	*Cruz Roja*	Red Cross (medical aid)
agua potable	drinking water	*cuesta*	slope
alto	high	*cueva*	cave
aparcamiento	parking	*cumbre*	summit
área recreativa	official picnic spot, usually with barbecues, toilets, water taps	*degollada*	pass
		derecha	right (direction)
		desprendimiento	landslide
		drago	'Dragon' Tree
arroyo	stream	*embalse*	reservoir
ayuntamiento	town hall	*era*	threshing circle
bajo	low	*ermita*	chapel
barranco	ravine	*Espacio*	
bocadillo	bread roll, snack	*Natural*	protected area of
bodegón	inn	*Protegido*	natural beauty
bosque	wood	*estación de*	
cabezo	peak, summit	*autobus/*	
cabra	goat	*guagua*	bus station
cabrera	goatherd	*farmacia*	chemist
calle	street	*faro*	lighthouse
camí	path or way	*fiesta*	holiday, celebration
camino	trail, path, track		
camino particular	private road	*finca*	farm, country house
camino real	old donkey trail (lit. royal road)	*fuente*	spring or source
		gasolinera	petrol station
campamento	camping	*guagua*	bus
carretera	main road	*Guanche*	original Canary Islands inhabitants
casa	house		
casa forestal	forestry house		
casa rural	country house, accommodation to let	*Guardia Civil*	police
		guía	guide
		hostal	hostel, accommodation
cascada	waterfall		
caserío	hamlet, village	*hoya*	depression (geological)
cementerio	cemetery		
centro de salud	health centre	*iglesia*	church
cerrado	closed	*información*	information
cerveza	beer	*isla*	island
choza	shack, hut	*izquierda*	left (direction)
clínica	clinic, hospital	*laurisilva*	ancient laurel forest
colegio	college, school		
comida	food	*lavadero*	laundry area

librería	bookshop	*puente*	bridge
llano	plain	*puerto*	port, mountain pass
lluvioso	rainy		
lomo	broad-backed ridge or spur dividing two valleys or ravines	*refugio*	refuge, shelter
		río	river, stream
		risco	crag or cliff
		roque	(a) lava fill exposed by erosion to form a broad, blunt pinnacle (b) rock
malpaís	'bad lands' wild, barren countryside		
mapa	map		
mercado	market	*ruta*	route
mirador	lookout/viewing point	*salida*	exit
		senda	path, track
montaña	mountain	*sendero*	foot path
nublado	cloudy	*sierra*	mountain range
nuevo	new	*sin salida*	no through road/route
oficina de turismo	tourist office		
		sirocco	hot, dust-laden wind from Africa
peligroso	dangerous		
pensión	guesthouse	*tapas*	bar snacks
pescado	fish	*tienda*	shop
pico	peak	*típico*	traditional bar/eating place
picón	black volcanic rock/sand		
		tormentoso	stormy
piscina	swimming pool	*torre*	tower
pista	dirt road/track	*torrente*	stream
pista forestal	forest road/track	*tubería*	water pipe
playa	beach	*valle*	valley
plaza	square	*vega*	meadow
policía	police	*ventoso*	windy
pozo	well	*viejo*	old
prohibido el paso	no entry	*zona recreativa*	recreation area